III

Sun Tzu's
Art of War
Playbook
Volume 3 of 9:
Opportunities

Gary Gagliardi

Sun Tzu's Art of War Playbook

Volume Three: Opportunities

by Gary Gagliardi
The Science of Strategy Institute
Clearbridge Publishing

Published by
Science of Strategy Institute, Clearbridge Publishing
    suntzus.com   scienceofstrategy.org

Library of Congress Control Number: 2014909969
First Print Edition
Also sold in ebook form as Sun Tzu's Warrior Rule Book
Copyright 2010, 2011, 2012, 2013, 2014 Gary Gagliardi
ISBN 9781929194780 (13-digit) 1929194781 (10-digit)

Originally published as a series of articles on the Science of Strategy Website, scienceofstratregy.org. and
later as an ebook on various sites.

PO Box 33772, Seattle, WA 98133
Phone: (206)542-8947 Fax: (206)546-9756
beckyw@clearbridge.com
garyg@scienceofstrategy.org

Manufactured in the United States of America.
Interior and cover graphic design by Dana and Jeff Wincapaw.
Original Chinese calligraphy by Tsai Yung, Green Dragon Arts, www.greendragonarts.com.

Publisher's Cataloging-in-Publication Data
Sun-tzu, 6th cent. B.C.
Opportunities, competition, success, decision-making
    [Sun-tzu ping fa, English]
    Art of War Playbook / Sun Tzu and Gary Gagliardi.
    p.197 cm. 23
    Includes introduction to basic competitive philosophy of Sun Tzu

Clearbridge Publishing's books may be purchased for business, for any promotional use,
or for special sales.

Contents

Playbook Overview

Note: This overview is provided for those who have not read the previous volume of Sun Tzu's Art of War Playbook. *It provides an brief overview of the work in general and the general concepts framing the first volume.*

Sun Tzu's **The Art of War** is less a "book" in the modern Western sense than it is an outline for a course of study. Like Euclid's Geometry, simply reading the work teaches us very little. Sun Tzu wrote in in a tradition that expected each line and stanza to be studied in the context of previous statements to build up the foundation for understanding later statements.

To make this work easier for today's readers to understand, we developed the **Strategy Playbook**, the Science of Strategy Institute (SOSI) guidebook to explaining Sun Tzu's strategy in the more familiar format of a series of explanations with examples. These lessons are framed in the context of modern competition rather than ancient military warfare.

This Playbook is the culmination of over a decade of work breaking down Sun Tzu's principles into a series of step-by-step practical articles by the Institute's multiple award-winning author and founder, Gary Gagliardi. The original *Art of War* was written for military generals who understood the philosophical concepts of ancient China, which in itself is a practical hurdle that most modern readers cannot clear. Our Art of War Playbook is written for today's reader. It puts Sun Tzu's ideas into everyday, practical language.

The Playbook defines a new science of strategic competition aimed at today's challenges. This science of competition is designed as the complementary opposite of the management science that is taught in most business schools. This science starts, as Sun Tzu did himself, by defining a better, more complete vocabulary for discussing competitive situations. It connects the timeless ideas of Sun Tzu to today's latest thinking in business, mathematics, and psychology.

The entire Playbook consists of two hundred and thirty articles describing over two-thousand interconnected key methods. These articles are organized into nine different areas of strategic skill from understanding positioning to defending vulnerabilities. All together this makes up over a thousand pages of material.

Playbook Access

The Playbook's most up-to-date version is available as separate articles on our website. Live links make it easy to access the connections between various articles and concepts. If you become a SOSI Member, you can access any Playbook article at any time and access their links.

However, at the request of our customers, we also offer these articles as a series of nine eBooks. Each of the nine sections of the entire Playbook makes up a separate eBook, Playbook Parts One Through Nine. These parts flow logically through the Progress Cycle of listen-aim-move-claim (see illustration). Because of the dynamic nature of the on-line version, these eBooks are not going to be as current as the on-line version. You can see a outline of current Playbook articles here and, generally, the eBook version will contain most of the same material in the same order.

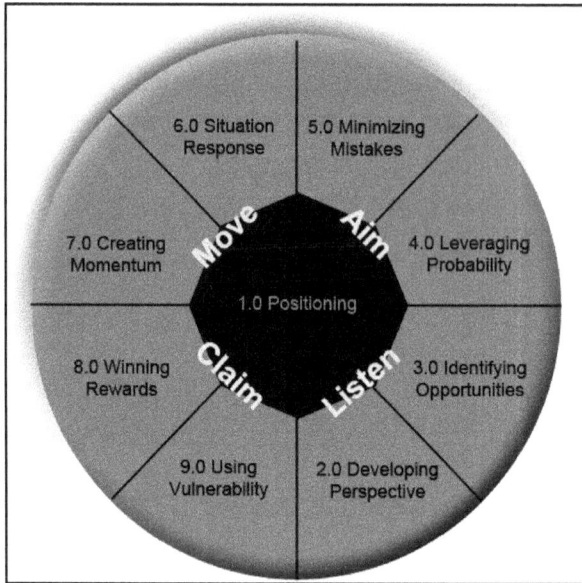

Nine categories of strategic skills define cycle that advances our positions:

1. Comparing Positions,

2. Developing Perspective,

3. Identifying Opportunities,

4. Leveraging Probability,

5. Minimizing Mistakes,

6. Responding To Situations,

7. Creating Momentum,

8. Winning Rewards, And

9. Defending Vulnerabilities.

Playbook Structure and Design

These articles are written in standard format including 1) the general principle, 2) the situation, 3) the opportunity, 4) the list of specific Art of War key methods breaking down the general principle into a series of actions, and 5) an illustration of the application of each of those key methods to a specific competitive situation. Key methods are written generically to apply to every competitive arena (business, personal life, career, sports, relationships, etc.) with each specific illustrations drawn from one of these areas.

A number identifies where each article appears in Playbook Structure. For example, the article 2.1.3 Strategic Deception is the third article in the first section of the second book in the nine volumes of the Strategy Playbook. In our on-line version, these links are live, clicking on them brings you to the article itself. We provide them because the interconnection of concepts is important in learning Sun Tzu's system.

Playbook Training

Training in Sun Tzu's warrior skills does not entail memorizing all these principles. Instead, these concepts are used to develop exercises and tools that allow trainees to put this ideas in practice. While each rule is useful, the heart of Sun Tzu system is the methods that connect all the principles together. Training in these principles is designed to develop a gut instinct for how Sun Tzu's strategy is used in different situations to produce success. Principles are interlinked because they describe a comprehensive conceptual mental model. Warrior Class training puts trainees in a situation where they must constantly make decisions, rewarding them for making decisions consist with winning productively instead of destructively.

About Positions

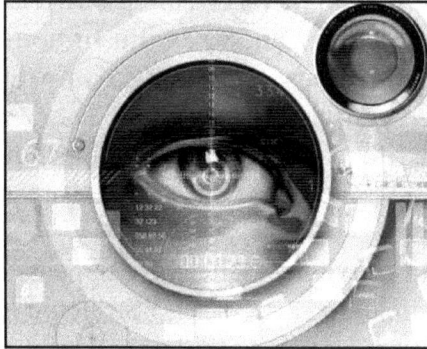

This first volume of Sun Tzu's Playbook focuses on teaching us the nature of strategic positions. "Position awareness" gives you a framework for understanding your strategic situation relative to the conditions around you. It enables you to see your position as part of a larger environment constructed of other positions and the raw elements that create positions. Master Sun Tzu's system of comparing positions, you can understand which aspect of your position are secure and which are the most dynamic and likely to change.

Traditional strategy defines a "position" as a comparison of situations. Game theory defines is as the current decision point that is arrive at as the sum or result of all previous decisions, both yours and those of others. Sun Tzu's methods of positioning awareness are different. They force you to see yourself in the eyes of others. Using these techniques, you broaden your perspective by gathering a range of viewpoints. In a limited sense, the scope of your position defines your area of control within your larger environment. In traditional strategy, five elements--mission, climate, ground, command, and methods--define the dimensions in which competitors can be compared.

Competition as Comparison

Sun Tzu saw that success is based on comparisons. This comparison must take place whenever a choice is made. For Sun Tzu, competition means a comparison of alternative choices or "positions". Battles are won by positioning before they are fought. These positions provide choices for everyone involved. Good positions discourage others from attacking you and invite them to support you. Sun Tzu's system teaches us how to systematically build up our positions to win success in the easiest way possible.

Competing positions are compared on the basis many elements, both objective and subjective. Sun Tzu's strategy is to identify these points of comparison and to understand how to leverage them. Learning Sun Tzu's strategy requires learning the details of how positions are compared and advanced. Sun Tzu taught that fighting to "sort things out" is a foolish way to find learn the strengths and weaknesses of a position. Conflict to tear down opposing positions is the most costly way to win competitive comparisons.

Today's More Competitive World

In the complex, chaotic world of today, we can easily get trapped into destructive rather than productive situations. Even our smallest decisions can have huge impact on our future. The problem is that we are trained for yesterday's world of workers, not today's world of warriors. We are trained in the linear thinking of planning in predictable, hierarchical world. This thinking applies less and less to today's networked, more competitive world.

Following a plan is the worker's skill of working in pre-defined functions in an internal, stable, controlled environment. The competitive strategy of Sun Tzu is the warrior's skill of making good decisions about conditions in complex, fast-changing, competitive environments. Sun Tzu's strategic system teaches us to adapt to the unexpected events that are becoming more and more common in our lives. We live in a world where fewer and fewer key events are planned. Navigating our new world of external challenges requires a different set of skills.

Most of us make our decisions without any understanding of competition. The result is that most of us lose as many battles as we win, never making consistent progress. Events buffet us, turning us in one direction and then the other. Too often, we end up repeating our past patterns of mistakes.

The Science of Strategy Institute teaches you the warrior's skills of adaptive response. There are many organizations that teach planning and organization. The Institute is one of the few places in the world you can get learn competitive thinking, and the only place in the world, with a comprehensive Playbook.

Seeing Situations Differently

Sun Tzu taught that a warrior's decision-making was a matter of reflex. As we develop our strategic decision-making skills, the critical conditions in situations simply "pop" out at us. This isn't magic. The latest research on how decisions are made tells us a lot about why Sun Tzu's principles work. It comes from using patterns to retrain our mind to see conditions differently. The study of successful response arose from military confrontations, where every battle clearly demonstrated how hard it is to predict events in the real world. Sun Tzu saw that winners were always those who knew how to respond appropriately to the dynamic nature of their situation.

Sun Tzu's principles provides a complete model for the key knowledge for understanding conditions in complex dynamic environments. This model "files" each piece of data into the appropriate place in the big picture. As the picture of your situation fills in, you can identify the opportunities hidden within your situation.

Making Decisions about Conditions

Instead of focusing on a series of planned steps, Sun Tzu's principles are about making decisions regarding conditions. It concerns itself with: 1) identifying the relative strengths and weaknesses of competitive positions, 2) advancing positions leveraging opportunities, and 3) the types of responses to specific challenges that work the most frequently. Using Sun Tzu's principles, we call these three areas position awareness , opportunity development , and situation response . Each area that we master broadens your capabilities.

- Position awareness trains us to recognize that competitive situations are defined by the relationship among alternative positions. Developing this perspective never ends. It deepens throughout our lives.
- Opportunity development explores the ground, testing our perceptions. Only testing the edges of perspective through action can we know what is true.
- S ituation response trains us to recognize the key characteristics of the immediate situation and to respond appropriately. Only by practice, can we learn to trust the viewpoint we have developed.

Success in competitive environments comes from making better decisions every day. Sharp strategic reflexes flow from a clear understanding of where and when you use which competitive tools methods.

The Key Viewpoints

As an individual, you have a unique and valuable viewpoint, but every viewpoint is inherently limited by its own position. The result is that people cannot get a useful perspective on their own situations and surrounding opportunities. The first formula of positioning awareness involve learning what information is relevant. The most advanced techniques teach how to gather that information and put it into a bigger picture.

Most people see their current situations as the sum of their past successes and failures. Too often people dwell on their mistakes while simultaneously sitting on their laurels. Sun Tzu's strategy forces you to see your position differently. How you arrived at your current position doesn't matter. Your position is what it is. It is shaped by history but history is not destiny.

In this framework, the only thing that matters is where you are going and how you are going to get there. As you begin to develop your strategic reflexes, you start to think more and more about how to secure your current position and advance it.

Seeing the Big Picture

Most people see all the details of their lives, but they cannot see what those detail mean in terms of the big picture. As you master position awareness, you don't see your life as a point but as a path. You see your position in terms of what is changing and what resources are available. You are more aware of your ability to make decisions and your skills in working with others.

Most importantly, this strategic system forces you to get in touch with your core set of goals and values.

Untrained people usually see their life in terms of absolutes: successes and failures, good luck and bad, weakness and strength. As you begin to master position awareness, you begin to see all comparisons of strength and weakness are temporary and relative. A position is not strong or weak in itself. Its strength or weakness depends on how it compares or "fits" with surrounding positions. Weakness and strength are not what a position is, but how you use it.

The Power of Perspective

Positional awareness gives you the specialized vocabulary you need to understanding how situations develop. Mastering this vocabulary, you begin to see the leverage points connecting past and future. You replace vague conceptions of "strength," "momentum," and "innovation" with much more pragmatic definitions that you can actually use on a day to day basis.

Mastering position awareness also changes your relationships with other people. It teaches you a different way of judging truth and character. This methods allow you to spot self-deception and dishonest in others. It also allows you to understand how you can best work with others to compensate for your different weaknesses.

Once you develop a good perspective of position, it naturally leads you to want to learn more about how you can improve you position through the various aspects of opportunity development covered in the subsequent parts of the Strategy Playbook.

Seeing the Invisible

The "Nazca lines" are giant drawings etched across thirty miles of desert on Peru's southern coast. The patterns are only visible at a distance of hundreds of feet in the air. Below that, they look like strange paths or roads to nowhere. Just as we cannot see these lines without the proper perspective, people who master Sun Tzu's methods can <u>suddenly recognize situations</u> that were invisible to them before. Unless we have the right perspective, we cannot compare situations and positions successfully. The most recent scientific research explains why people cannot see these patterns for comparison without developing the network framework of adaptive thinking.[1]

Seeing Patterns

We can imagine patterns in chaotic situations, but seeing real pattern is the difference between success and failure. In our seminars, we demonstrate the power of seeing patterns in a number of exercises.

The <u>mental models</u> used by warrior give them "situation awareness." This situation awareness isn't just vague theory. Recent research shows that it can be measured in a variety of ways.[2] We now know that untrained people fall victim to a flow of confusing information because they don't know where its pieces fit. Those trained in Sun Tzu's mental models plug this stream of information quickly and easily into a bigger picture, transforming the skeleton's provided by Sun Tzu's system into a functioning awareness of your strategic position and its relation to other positions. Each piece of information has a place in that picture. As the information comes in, it fills in the picture, like pieces of a puzzle.

The ability to see the patterns in this bigger picture allows experts in strategy to see what is invisible to most people in a number of ways. They include:

- People trained in Art of War principles--<u>recognition-primed decision-making</u> --see patterns that others do not.
- Trained people can spot anomalies, things that should happen in the network of interactions but don't.
- Trained people are in touch with changes in the environment within appropriate time horizons.
- Trained people recognize complete patterns of interconnected elements under extreme time pressure.

Procedures Make Seeing Difficult

One of the most surprising discoveries from this research is that those who know procedures, that is, a linear view of events, alone have a ***more*** difficult time recognizing patterns than novices. An interesting study[3] examined the different recognition skills of three groups of people 1) experts, 2) novices, and 3) trainers who taught the standard procedures. The three groups were asked to pick out an expert from a group novices in a series of videos showing them performing a decision-making task, in this case, CPR. Experts were able to recognize the expert 90% of the time. Novices recognized the expert 50% of the time. The shocking fact was that trainers performed much worse that the novices, recognizing the expert only 30% of the time.

Why do those who know procedures fail to see what the experts usually see and even novices often see? Because, as research into <u>mental simulations</u> has shown, those with only a procedural model fit everything into that model and ignore elements that don't fit. In the above experiment, interviews with the trainers indicated that they assumed that the experts would always follow the procedural model. In real life, experts adapt to situations where unique conditions often trump procedure. Adapting to the situation rather than following set procedures is a central focus the form of strategy that the Institute teaches.

Missing Expected Elements

People trained to recognize the bigger picture beyond procedures also recognize when expected elements are missing from the picture. These anomalies or, what the cognition experts [4] describe as "negative cues" are invisible to novices *and* to those trained only in procedure. Without sense of the bigger pattern, people are focused too narrowly on the problem at hand. The "dog that didn't bark" from the Sherlock Holmes story, "Silver Blaze," is the most famous example of a negative cue. Only those working from a larger nonprocedural framework can expect certain things to happen and notice when they don't.

The ability to see what is missing also comes from the expectations generated by the mental model. Process-oriented models have the expectation of one step following another, but situation-recognition models create their expectations from signals in the environment. Research [5] into the time horizons of decision-makers shows that different time scales are at work. People at the highest level of organizations must look a year or two down the road, using strategic models that work in that timeframe, doing strategic planning. Decision-makers on the front-lines, however, have to react within minutes or even seconds to changes in their situation, working from their strategic reflexes. The biggest danger is that people get so wrapped up in a process that they lose contact with their environment.

Decisions Under Pressure

Extreme time pressure is what distinguishes front-line decision-making from strategic planners. One of the biggest discoveries in cognitive research [6] is that trained people do much better in seeing their situation instantly and making the correct decisions under time pressure. Researchers found virtually no difference between the decisions that experts made under time pressure when comparing them to decisions made without time pressure. That research also finds that those with less experience and training made dramatically worse decisions when they were put under time pressure.

The central argument for training our strategic reflexes is that our situation results, not from chance or luck, but from <u>the instant decisions</u> that that we all make every day. Our position is the sum of these decisions. If we cannot make the right decisions on the spot, when they are needed, our plans usually come to nothing. This is why we describe training people's strategic reflexes as helping them "do at first what most people only do at last."

The success people experience seeing what is invisible to others is dramatic. To learn more about how the strategic reflexes we teach differ from what can be planned, read about <u>the contrast between planning and reflexes here</u> . As <u>our many members report</u>, the success Sun Tzu's system makes possible is remarkable.

1 Chi, Glaser, & Farr, 1988, The Nature of Expertise, Erlbaum
2 Endsley & Garland, Analysis and Measurement of Situation Awareness
3 Klein & Klein, 1981, "Perceptual/Cognitive Analysis of proficient CPR Performance", Midwestern Psychological Association Meeting, Chicago.
4 Dr. David Noble, Evidence Based Research, Inc.In Gary Klein, Sources of Power, 1999
5 Jacobs & Jaques, 1991, "Executive Leadership".In Gal & Mangelsdofs (eds.), Handbook of Military Psychology, Wiley
6 Calder, Klein, Crandall,1988, "Time Pressure, Skill, and Move Quality in Chess". American Journal of Psychology, 101:481-493

About Opportunities

Competition is a comparison. People must compare alternatives before they can make choices. Potential supporters must compare before they can choose to work with you. You must compare before you can make choices about what opportunities to pursue.

Our last formula focussed on collecting better information for comparison. After collecting information, you use that information in this chapter's formula to identify opportunities.

This raises the serious question: what is an opportunity? The simplest definition is an opening in the environment into which you can expand and build up your position. You can only move into that space if it is open. This is why we use the term opening to describe strategic opportunities.

Success requires improving your position, moving from one opportunity to a better one. To move forward, you must find opportunities. These openings are stepping-stones to success. The Observe Opportunities Formula reveals the right times, proper conditions, and best places to find opportunities.

The Opportunity in Openings

To make progress, you need an opening. Openings are empty spaces in the environment. They are areas that are being overlooked by competitors. These spaces are not empty because of what you do or do not do. They are empty because of what everyone else is doing or not doing.

Sun Tzu states his view of the nature of opportunities simply:

> *You see the opportunity for victory; you don't control it.*
> The Art of War, 4:1:10

This short phrase raises three important points that you should understand about opportunities before proceeding.

The competitive environment creates and controls opportunities. Changes in the climate create opportunities. Openings are conditions in the environment. You do not control conditions in the environment. The environment is very large. The largest organization is microscopic by comparison. Thinking that you can create an opportunity in the environment is like a drop of water thinking that it can change the tides of the ocean.

Sun Tzu's principles teaches you to see opportunities, not to create them. Recognizing opportunities is difficult enough because an opportunity looks like nothing. Once you see opportunities, you can compare them. Creating opportunities is impossible. If you try to create opportunities, you are wasting your time and resources. You must use those resources to pursue opportunities that the forces in your environment create.

Finally, you cannot create opportunity. To become successful, you can create a campaign. You can create a position for an organization in the competitive environment. In Sun Tzu's Art of War Playbook, we have key methods for creating communication networks, momentum, sales, and lots of other valuable stuff for improving positions. When you think about what you can create, you must think about what takes advantage of existing opportunities. Before you can know what to create, you must recognize those opportunities.

Openings are like a black hole. There isn't anything to see. There are no competitors, no products, mo obvious resources, and no money being made in them. You cannot see nothing. Like a black hole, we must recognize an opening by what it happening around it.

The Choice Between Offense and Defense

Your first responsibility is to defend your existing position. Competition is a game you can only play while you have resources. When you run out, the game is over. Income from resources the lifeblood of an enterprise. You must preserve existing sources of income. You only look for new areas to conquer when your current base is secure.

Successful advances are like climbing a ladder. You gradually shift your weight from one rung to the next. The rule is that you move into new area quickly, but you abandon old bases slowly. In emergencies, you can be forced to move because your existing position has fallen apart, but normally you preserve your existing sources of revenue as you advance.

If your existing position is resource poor, you have to work more carefully. If moving into new positions hollows out your existing position, such a move can be fatal. In this situation, you focus less on external opportunities in the environment and more on internal opportunities in your systems. You need less strategy and more planning. Instead of looking for openings in the environment, you look for openings within your systems to control your expenses. As your systems improve, you eventually have more resources than you need to preserve your existing revenue stream. This is when you move into new opportunities in the environment.

Many organizations get this process backward. When their existing organizations are doing well, they devote their excess resources to internal systems, but they neglect pursuing new opportunities. They wait until their existing positions are in trouble before considering new opportunities. Putting more resources into profitable operations can be necessary to support growth, but frequently you are working at the wrong end of the law of diminishing returns. For every additional effort and dollar you put in, you are going to get less and less of a return.

People tend to let necessity dictate their attempts at advance. For example, people look for a new job at the worst possible time: when they are out of work. You are much more successful if you counter this tendency. It is a hundred times easier to find a new job when you are doing well in your existing job. It is also a hundred times easier to pursue new opportunities when your existing position is doing well.

New opportunities are more plentiful than most people think, but the best opportunities do not come on any schedule. Because of this, you must protect and build up your existing position and wait patiently until a new opportunity appears. When a new opportunity appears, you must let your existing position take care of itself while you concentrate on your advance.

Where to Look for Opportunity

You never fight competitors in the environment directly or try to control the environment. The environment is bigger than both you and your competitors. There are right ways and wrong ways to deal with the competition. The worst approach is to target a competitor's strong points.

The most common strategic mistake is to simply copy competitors who already dominate an environment. Imitation works in specific competitive situations that we cover later, but the success of your competitors in an environment never defines an opportunity.

What happens when you directly attack established competitors? You discover that you cannot make their position your own. You can try to duplicate their systems and contacts. You can try to offer a product that is superior in every way. You still won't win their supporters. This seems unfair, but it is the way it is. You can't let this frustrate and anger you. You can't change it by wasting money on marketing. All competitors must create their own unique positions. Trying to destroy the positions of others is a disaster.

People naturally follow the crowd. This is especially true in business, where every business tries to copy the latest popular product or idea. This never works because crowded areas create unprofitable positions. Following the crowd to find an opportunity is like trying to feed yourself on the scraps other leave.

If you want to be successful, go after empty spaces—openings—not areas that are already crowded. You must see openings in your environment and fill them before competitors recognize them. The power of this concept is that it moves you away from conflict with competitors. It moves you into areas where you can win their support without fighting them. It puts you in control because you are always picking your own supporters.

Your competitors can be well entrenched in their positions. You cannot beat them by going after their positions directly, succeeding in the same way that they do. Even though you share your competitive space or neighborhood with them, you must see the space differently than they do. You don't look at what competitors are doing. You look at what they are failing to do.

You don't want to fight your competitors for position. Battling over position is never profitable, even if you win. No matter how dominant your competitors are, some of their supporters are unhappy. This is certain because no one can do everything well. When you recognize this unhappiness and its cause, you are well on the path to finding your opportunity.

The bigger the organization, the more powerful the position, the more certain it is that that position has unhappy supporters. You must focus on the supporters that competitors have served the most poorly, the needs that they leave unsatisfied. Supporters choose you because you have first chosen them. When you choose to target a group of supporters, you choose to fill a particular type of need. The larger your competitors are, the more supporters they are trying to satisfy and the more specific needs they must neglect.

Competitors may be bigger, but if they are focused on satisfying the demands of their position how can their size hurt you? The larger their base of supporters, the more likely it is that some of those people are unhappy.

You beat competitors, no matter how large, by choosing where and when you compete. Positions that seem difficult are really easy when you understand the power of choice. Your choices control how much competition you have. You can divide the areas of competition to define where you compete best. You can fulfill the supporters' needs that competitors do not address.

Some competitors will always be much bigger than you are, but this means that they have many areas in which they can invest their resources. You want them to spread themselves too thin. You can then choose the opening that you want to address. You target supporters who are well suited to your mission and skills. You choose supporters whom your opponent has ignored because their needs are poorly suited to your competitor's mission and skill.

If competitors work globally, you focus locally. If they offer broad appeals, you can offer customized ones. If they deal in large volumes, you can offer more specialized releases. If they use standard terms, you can create special ones. The list goes on and on.

Your much larger, richer, more professional, more experienced competitors will continually overlook opportunities that are right under their noses. How can they hit a target that they cannot see?

You control where you compete. Your competition cannot control you unless you let them.

Sun Tzu's principles teach that strength can be a source of weakness. Only by studying the known strengths of competitors can you see where they are creating opportunities. All strengths create a complementary weakness. You must see how to put your strengths against your competitors' weaknesses.

Your competitors can have all types of different strengths. It doesn't matter what those strengths are. No one does everything well. People have to choose where to focus their resources. When they choose what strengths to develop, they are also choosing to develop weaknesses elsewhere.

Strength and weakness are another pair of those complementary opposites. Strength and weakness are two sides of the same condition. You discover opponents' weaknesses by studying their strengths.

This is simpler than it may sound at first.

For example, if a business focuses on having the lowest price, they must sacrifice some aspect of quality. If they focus on high quality, they are vulnerable on price. If they focus on doing specific things extremely well, they perform a broad range of services poorly. If they focus on a broad range of services, they lose the ability to perfect any one of those services. If they emphasize standards and speed, they must de-emphasize customization and personal service.

Whatever competitors do well, they are leaving an opening for you to do the opposite. Instead of envying their strengths, you can turn those strengths into weaknesses. Their packaging is more professional? Aim for a more natural look. Everyone knows who they are? Emphasize that only the select few know to work with you. If competitors attempt everything, they will do everything poorly and they will leave openings everywhere.

The truth is that human needs and tastes are infinite. All supporters have unmet needs. Solving one set of needs creates another. You pick your opportunities to address unmet needs. All competitors offer specific solutions. They cannot satisfy every customer.

The Role of Focus

If you look for opportunities arising from a competitors' strengths, you work their blind spots. If you target more obvious weaknesses, your competitors are already working to address these shortcomings. Your competitors must not recognize the opening that you see as an opportunity. You don't want to pin your hopes on weaknesses that they plan to address. You want to use opportunities that they cannot address without undermining their strengths.

You must keep your desire to leverage their strengths against them a secret. You don't want them to recognize their strengths as weaknesses. Don't give your competitors any ideas. They will be confident in their strengths if you don't draw their attention.

As you move toward these positions, do it quietly without competitors noticing. Do not let your competitors know what you are up to. Keep quiet about what you are doing. Make sales quietly. Avoid the media. Communicate to supporters directly so your competitors can't make adjustments to your moves.

You want to be assured that those to whom you are compared are too distracted to care about winning the supporters you target. You also don't want them trying to win those supporters back before you make them yours. This means that you have to know where competitors are planning to move in the future. You should know what new positions they are developing and in which positions they plan to expand.

The new plans divert competitors' limited attention from their existing supporters. Where competitors divide their attention, they create openings. If you know where they are expanding, you also know who they are forgetting. Focus your venture on gaps in their attention.

When you focus on a small area to develop your position among a limited group of supporters, you concentrate your resources. You must focus all your efforts into areas competitors serve poorly. You can then put a lot of resources into areas where others have put few. You can easily do a better job there than your much larger competitors.

In business, for example, your competitor's problem customers are not your problem customers. People tend to avoid problems, especially other people's problems, but your competitors' problems are not your problems. A few of your competitors' problems are your opportunities.

Problems are created by unsatisfied needs. Unsatisfied needs are openings. They are the true emptiness that creates opportunities. Every one of those needs points to an opening, an opportunity. To be skilled in finding opportunities, you must search out problems that others have left unresolved.

We all know that success come from satisfying people's needs, but we still don't recognize the opportunities hidden in every problem. Just like people thoughtlessly miss opportunities by following the crowd, most people miss opportunities by avoiding problems.

How can you tell if a competitor's problem is your opportunity? You have to consider how well those unmet needs match your mission, your resources, and your time constraints. Competitors leave gaps in the market because they cannot do everything well. However, you cannot do everything well either. You want to aggressively fill the gaps that competitors leave when those gaps fit your own resources.

You must be selective about what opportunities you pursue. You want to ask yourself three questions. Does satisfying these unmet needs meet your organization's mission? How well does the problem space match your resources? Will you solve the problem first?

You develop a mission to help you select the opportunities. If you are true to your mission, you will become better and better at solving a particular kind of problems.

Resource fit combines your enterprise's skills with your excess capacity. Your enterprise must have the right amount of excess resources to address the size of the market. The type of barriers blocking the opening must be well suited to your personal skills and your enterprise's systems. You must be able to easily contact the market and provide it a solution. If you cannot do both, the resource fit is not right.

Your affinity and proximity to the problem must give you a first-mover advantage. The best preparation for winning a market position is getting to the market first. In some market spaces, this is the single most important issue.

If you get to a market first, then you have time to build up your position and lay traps for your competitors. Since they are playing catch-up, it is easy to exhaust your new competitors. You can drain rich competitors. You can even push around bigger competitors. Didn't I say that strategy was fun?

Learn from the history of successful ventures. Success goes to those who make progress easy. Your ideal customer is one who is inexpensive to win. You don't have to become famous to win new positions. You also don't have to take chances in winning supporters.

You must engage only in successful campaigns. Find supporters that you can easily satisfy. Never pass by an opening that makes competitors look bad.

If an opportunity doesn't really play to my strengths, can I develop new skills to take advantage of it?

If you cannot see an opening that clearly fit your abilities, you must not move. You cannot always find a new opportunity. They may be there, but if you don't see them, be patient. You will eventually discover new opportunities. Then you can advance.

You must only go after positions that you are sure you can win. Avoid positions that are too large for you to dominate. Go after positions that are small enough for you to fill completely. You must have the resources to campaign for these positions. Go after a position when you have an easy solution to the problem that shapes it. Avoid crowded environments. Look for positions where you have a first mover advantage. Until then, you must conserve your resources so that you have plenty of ammunition when the right opportunity appears.

You may see new positions that you would like to win. However, you may not see an affordable solution for those situations. This means the opportunity isn't quite right. You may see how to win new positions by spending a lot of money. This also shows that the problem is not an opportunity.

You want to move into new positions effortlessly. You must avoid risking your current positions. Wait for the right time to move. Don't try to be too clever. Learning about potential opportunities is easy if you listen to your contact network. Don't imagine opportunities where you want them.

Success only requires enough faith to believe that people have an endless supply of problems. You will eventually observe opportunities that you can win without effort. Avoid highly competitive situations. Invest resources only if it is clear that a market can be profitable. You will succeed if you avoid making hasty decisions.

You build a great organization by first finding the right supporters. Only then do you worry about investing resources. Find the right supporters for your position and then invest only in what you absolutely need to win them.

3.0.0 Identifying Opportunities

Description: Sun Tzu's five key methods regarding the use of opportunities to advance a position.

"You can recognize the opportunity for victory; you don't create it."

Sun Tzu's The Art of War 4:1:1

"The reason so many people never get anywhere in life is because when opportunity knocks, they are out in the backyard looking for four-leaf clovers."

Walter Percy Chrysler

General Principle: A strategic perspective requires systematically gathering outside opinions and facts.

Situation:

This problem is identifying opportunities. One of the most common strategic mistakes is thinking that we have to duplicate the strengths of others in order to be competitive. The race goes to the swiftest. To win, we must be the fastest. However, strategic contests are more complicated than contests of skill. In competitive positioning, we seldom find opportunities duplicating the success of others. The opposite, finding success by focusing on the weaknesses of others, is the general rule.

Opportunity:

In normal usage, we use the word "opportunity" to describe any situation that offers an advantage or a combination of favorable circumstances. In Sun Tzu's strategy, we use the term "opportunity" to specifically to describe an opening in the direction of our goal. If we think in terms of advancing our position, openings allow us to move forward easily. Like all of strategy, an opening arises from a simple comparison (1.3.1 Competitive Comparison). An opening represents a vacant position that is relatively better than our current one. That position must be "open" because we don't want to get into contests to take positions away from those who already control them. These conflicts of strength against strength are just too expensive (3.1.3 Conflict Cost).

Key Methods:

To find opportunities, we must understand what they are and how they are created. The most basic key methods are:

1. Strategic economics dictates pursuing openings in our environment. No position is perfect. Relatively better positions offer a better balance of costs and rewards. Openings reflect unfulfilled needs in the environment. There are many specific types of costs and rewards, but, by pursuing openings, we avoid the most predictable cost, that of conflict and pursue the most predictable source of reward, the needs of others (3.1.0 Strategic Economics).

2. Opportunities are constantly created and destroyed by the natural shifts in needs. Once an opening is filled, a need satisfied, the opportunity is no longer there but moves somewhere else.

Phases such as a "window of opportunity" express our common sense appreciation for this.

3. Opportunities are generated by the natural dynamics of the competitive environment. No one creates their own opportunities. All we can do is position ourselves correctly to be in the right place at the right time when openings occur. Opportunity creation follows a pattern. We learn to recognize where opportunities are being created (3.2 Opportunity Creation).

4. *An opportunity is only an opportunity if we have the resources to pursue it.* Pursuing opportunities without understanding the constraints of our limited can be extremely dangerous. All openings are opportunities for someone, but we are interesting only in openings that represent *our* opportunities (3.3 Opportunity Resources).

5. *Large competitors create lots of opportunities smaller organizations.* One of the most common reasons that we fail to recognize opportunities is that we tend to think of size as an advantage. Large organizations reshape the environment in ways that create openings and opportunities for smaller competitors. In competitive arenas, size advantages turn into weaknesses that we can exploit (3.4 Dis-Economies of Scale).

6. *A strength or fullness in one area points to the opportunity in a corresponding weakness or emptiness in another.* Nature abhors a vacuum. We think of this emptiness as an unfulfilled need. Needs are vacuums that want to be filled. The ideal battleground is one that is empty but needs to be filled because of the nature of the opening. The most non-intuitive principles in strategy relate to how this emptiness creates wealth and power (3.5 Strength and Weakness).

7. *Opportunities are hard to see because they sit in gaps in our perception.* We cannot see openings because there is nothing to see. We see success, but success is what happens when someone fills an opening. We develop mental models that allow us to see the gap between objective reality and our subjective impressions of it to find opportunities (3.6 Leveraging Subjectivity).

8. We can discover opportunities by redefining the nature of the ground. Competition is based on making comparisons. The problem is that there are just some types of comparisons in which we are never going to look as good as we can. How comparisons are made is based upon a subjective decision. This choice either divides one set of contestants or one set of judges from another. This choice defines the advantageous "battle ground" (3.7 Defining the Ground).

9. We can see opportunities by mapping the five key elements. There are many types of openings, but we miss many of our potential opportunities because we cannot "see" the concepts involved. Given the right techniques, we can map the five dimensions used in Sun Tzu's strategic analysis into a two-dimensional picture (3.8 Strategic Matrix Analysis).

10. Illustration:

Let us use some business examples from the Internet to illustrate what opportunities are.

1. Strategic economics dictates pursuing openings in our environment. Yahoo, Google, PayPal, YouTube, Twitter, and all the other Internet companies found needs that no one else had satisfied on the newly created ground of the web.

2. Opportunities are constantly created and destroyed by the natural shifts in needs. The advantage that newspapers held since the invention of the printing press faded as electronic media rose. It simply uses less resources to deliver news and information via the Internet. Google saw that the business advantage of the Internet was in advertising. As buyer's eyes moved from papers to the Internet, sellers needed advertising to reach them. Old media dies. New media is born. *An opportunity is only an opportunity if we have the resources to pursue it.* The old media didn't have the intellectual resources to provide their customers with an entry into the new media. Time/Warner saw the opportunity. Time/Warner tried to get into the Internet by purchasing AOL, but they lack the intellectual resources do master the new area. Google had the intellectual resources of a new search algorithm and was the first to connect advertising with searching. *Large competitors create lots of opportunities smaller organizations.* The culture of a large media organizations didn't allow it to adapt to the rapidly changing environment of the internet. Time/Warner/AOL at legitimized the new media and created opportunities for much smaller competitors. Those competitors rose up to eventually swamp the much larger company.

3. A strength or fullness in one area points to the opportunity in a corresponding weakness or emptiness in another. The vast number of places offering text information on the Internet created

4. an opening for the video information provided by YouTube. The detailed information on the internet created a need for brief information more suitable to phones offered by Twitter. *Opportunities are hard to see because they sit in gaps in our perception.* In a retail environment, we see shopping and buying as the same general process. The difference between the two processes becomes clearer on the Internet. We shop to learn what we want. We buy to get the best price and service.

5. We can discover opportunities by redefining the nature of the ground. The division between shopping and buying has created a host of new opportunities for both shopping services where we learn, such as C/Net for information on electronics, and buying services where we save such as Amazon.

6. We can see opportunities by mapping the five key elements. Using the matrix analysis, we can see both where the various competitors on the Internet sit and where potential openings are. *Knowledge value and secrecy go hand in hand, both requiring the other.* We must know which information that we need to communicate to attract customers and which information we must keep secret to maintain a competitive advantage.

3.1.0 Strategic Economics

Description: Sun Tzu's six key methods balancing the cost and benefits of positioning.

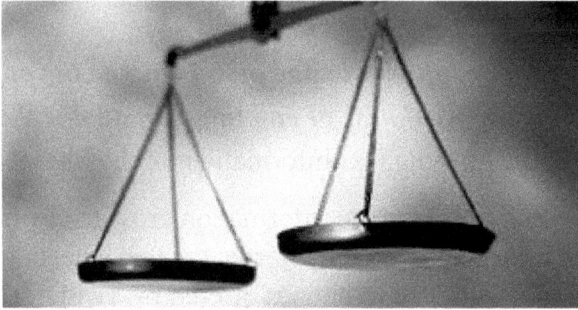

"Many advantages add up to victory. Few advantages add up to defeat."

Sun Tzu's The Art of War 1:5:5-6

"Wise men profit more from fools than fools from wise men; for the wise men shun the mistakes of fools, but fools do not imitate the successes of the wise."

Cato the Elder

General Principle: We must engage in only productive moves not destructive ones.

Situation:

Sun Tzu's competitive strategy is based on simple economics. One of the most destructive human tendencies is our ability to mentally separate the advantages of a position from its disadvantages, its benefits from its costs. The wost aspect of this tendency making decision on the basis of benefits without concerning ourselves with costs. Sun Tzu uses positioning to avoid wars of attrition because such wars are costly and "winning" does not assure a real pay-off. Decisions have consequences and all decisions have costs. Even deciding not to act has costs, the costs of missing opportunity. Experience has shown that the most costly decisions of all are those that focus on only benefits.

Opportunity:

Sun Tzu's competitive methods teach us to make profitable decisions. These decisions consistently yield more benefits than their costs. This can be more difficult than it seems. We start with the habit of seeing costs and benefit as two sides of the same coin. This thinking is ingrained into aspects of Sun Tzu's system because of its basis on Yin-Yang Philosophy. We call this concept complementary opposites. It teaches that the real world situations exist as a balance of opposing forces (3.2.3 Complementary Opposites). In economics, balancing costs and benefits is considered the basis of rational thinking. We study Sun Tzu to make this approach instinctive so all decisions are automatically based upon the balance without conscious consideration.

Key Methods:

The economics of Sun Tzu's competitive strategy are based on six general key methods.

1. Strategic economics always looks at our resources as strictly limited. Our decisions must take into account and make the most of these limited resources. Our most limited is our time, which means that even delaying a decision has a cost (3.1.1 Resource Limitations).

2. Profitable strategic economics requires separating what is knowable and what is not. Some things we can know for certain, such as the fact that our resources are limited. Other things, such as likely responses, we can know only as probabilities. Other things are simply unknowable before we make a decision. Making profitable decisions requires clearly separating these various realms of knowledge (3.1.2 Strategic Profitability).

3. Strategic economics always sees the biggest source of certain costs as conflict. Conflict means moving directly against opposition, especially fighting with them for positions. Conflict is always costly. While winning through conflict can put us on top temporarily, it always weakens us. If we improved our position by making ourselves weaker, we only invite more attacks. We face an unending supply of potential rivals. If we try to maintain our position through conflict, any seeming victory is strictly temporary. While we cannot know its costs exactly, we can always know that conflict is more costly than avoiding conflict. This may be the most non-intuitive of Sun Tzu's key methods. This is why so many decisions lead to disaster (3.1.3 Conflict Cost).

4. Strategic economics always uses openings to avoid costly conflict. An opening is not only absence of opposition but an empty position that nature rewards us to fill. Staying on top requires that the environment itself support us. An opening is inexpensive for us to fill because it generates more resources than it consumes (3.1.4 Opposition Openings).

5. Strategic economics teaches that neither the cost nor the value of pursuing a given opportunity can be predicted precisely. This means that we must make mistakes in calculating strategic profitability. This means that **all** of our decisions must minimize costs, avoiding fatal errors that consume our resources. We cannot predict costs so we must control them (3.1.5 Economic Unpredictability).

6. Strategic economics insists that the ultimate economic restriction is always time. Our current position is our source of our resources. We need excess resources, more than what we need to maintain our position, to pursue new opportunities. How quickly we can and must act and how long a campaign we can entertain depend on those economics. The longer we wait to move, the more our existing position can degrade over time, producing diminishing resources. The more opportunities we miss by waiting, the less opportunities we have left in the future (3.1.6 Time Limitations).

Illustration:

We often compare good strategy to a game like Go rather than a game like chess. Chess is designed as a war of attrition, where victory goes to the last person standing. Go is a game of building up positions, where victory goes to the person who is the most efficient in building up his or her position over time.

1. ***Strategic economics always looks at our resources as strictly limited.*** In chess, we have a limited number of pieces. In GO, a limited number of places on the board. As pieces or positions are "consumed" we get no more of them.

2. ***Profitable strategic economics requires separating what is knowable and what is not.*** We can know the key methods for placing pieces. We can know what our opponent has done in the past. We cannot know what either our opponents will do in the future or how we will respond.

3. ***Strategic economics always sees the biggest source of certain costs as conflict.*** While both of these games force conflict because of their limitations, we constantly avoid conflict because we cannot exactly predict its results. In chess, a forced exchange of pieces changes the situation so much that it can have implications that are impossible for us to foresee. In GO, we waste positions by continually challenging an opponent's moves instead of building our own positions.

4. ***Strategic economics always uses openings to avoid costly conflict.*** In both chess and GO, the openings are moves that we can make without forcing conflict. In both games, good moves open up our position to more open moves while pinning down our opponents to fewer open moves.

5. ***Strategic economics teaches that neither the cost nor the value of pursuing a given opportunity can be predicted precisely.*** All the possible paths in the future are more than we can foresee. The number of possible moves in a single game of chess exceeds the number of particles in the universe.

6. Strategic economics insists that the ultimate economic restriction is always time. In any strategic games like Go or chess, the winner is always concerned about wasting moves. A wasted move is a move that can be easily reversed by an opponent. In the end, the winner is the player who makes the most moves advancing his or her position that cannot be reversed.

3.1.1 Resource Limitations

Description: Sun Tzu's six key methods regarding the inherent limitation of strategic resources.

"If you exhaust your wealth, you then quickly hollow out your military."

Sun Tzu's The Art of War 2:3:5

"Genius has limitations; stupidity is boundless."

Anonymous

General Principle: Each of the five elements of a postition provides different resources and different limitations.

Situation:

Competitive decisions are choices about how to use limited resources. Our decisions often squander our limited resources. Most of us don't understand 1) what strategic resources are, 2) how they are limited, and 3) how they are consumed. Economic resources, such as money or property, make up only one of the five categories of strategic resources. Each category of resources is inherently limited, but they are limited in different ways. Some are consumed by using them. Others are multiplied by using them. Some are consumed by doing something. Others are consumed by doing nothing.

Opportunity:

When we understand the true nature of a strategic position, we get a much clearer understanding of what strategic resources are. Each of the five elements that makeup a position contributes a type of critical resource (1.3 Elemental Analysis). To understand our opportunities, we must see these resources more clearly, what these resources are and how they can be unintentionally wasted. Once we recognize their value, we are much more likely to protect our resources (1.1.2 Defending Positions). The mental models of strategy are devised to enable us to recognize not only the five major categories of resources but all their many different characteristics.

Key Methods:

We get our resources from our current position. Each of the five elements that define a position (mission, climate, ground, leader, and methods) define a different major category of resources. These resources are what we use to advance our position.

1. Values are the limited resources that we get from our mission. We need values to find supporters. Promoting goals and values that others cannot share destroys this resource. Our values allow us to join with others for our mutual benefit. We must choose one set of values. To do that, we must reject other sets of values. The refusal to choose values is the rejection of all values (1.6 Mission Values).

2. Limited temporary resources come from the climate aspect of our climate position. The key temporary resources are time and trends. All temporary resources expire over time. We are limited to only 24 hours in a day, but we use them up each day no matter what we do. Temporary resources are easier to waste because they expire simply by not using them. The problem with killing time is that it will kill us right back (1.4.1 Climate Shift).

3. Limited physical resources are what we get from our ground position. These include both our economic and social resources. Our material resources are limited. We can only have so much money, space, and connections with others. The ground offers a tremendous variety of resources, but they are all limited because we control limited ground ((1.4.2 Ground Features).

4. Limited character resources come from our decision-making capabilities. Strategy defines five types of character resources--courage, discipline, trustworthiness, caring, and intelligence. While all these reservoirs of character are limited, we need these limitations of character. The danger in terms of decision making in an excess of resources in these five areas. Too much courage leads to foolhardiness. Too much discipline to rigidity. (1.5.1 Command Leadership).

5. Limited skills and reputation are the resources we get from methods. Skill and reputation are just the objective and subjective sides of the same coin. No one can know how to do everything. However, unlike other resources, the more we use our skills and reputations, the more of them we develop. Their limitations come from outside. Our values, time, ground, character limit the type and number of skills we can master. Working outside of those limitations is costly and dangerous (1.5.2. Group Methods).

6. *No matter how many resources we have, the environment always has incalculably more.* People together are always much more powerful than individuals. All the resources of the most powerful person in the world are minuscule when compared with the power of the world as a whole. If we do not leverage our resources with opportunities created by the environment, those resources are wasted. One of the reasons that we seek to advance our position is to increase our resources, but no matter how far we advance, our resources are still limited and still insignificant in terms of controlling the environment as a whole, but more resources allow us to extend our control further and further (3.2.1 Environmental Dominance).

Illustration:

Let us look at the problem with limitations of resources from the aspect of someone pursuing a career in sports.

1. Values are the limited resources that we get from our mission. If a player thinks more of his or her own success and stats than the success of the team, their support within the team will decline.

2. Limited temporary resources come from the climate aspect of our climate position. As a player gets older, their abilities can grow or decline depending how they use their time, but no matter what they do, their careers are limited in terms of their ability to play the game.

3. Limited physical resources are what we get from our ground position. A player's natural physical abilities come from the nature of their body but those skills no matter how great are limited in many ways. Also, no matter how much money a player makes, he or she can still get into financial trouble.

4. Limited character resources come from our decision-making capabilities. A player with all the physical abilities in the world can get into trouble because of character flaws. Those flaws affect his or her decisions on and off the field.

5. Limited skills and reputation are the resources we get from methods. A player can master new skills as time goes on. A player with the right character and use of their time, can move from playing to coaching.

6. *No matter how many resources we have, the environment always has incalculably more.* The greatest player in history is eventually overshadowed by a newer player. Time provides a steady stream of new players and eventually one of them will surpass any past player in any given category (unless the games changes beyond comparison).

3.1.2 Strategic Profitability

Description: Sun Tzu's nine key methods for understanding gains and losses.

"Make no assumptions about all the dangers in using military force. Then you won't make assumptions about the benefits of using arms either."
Sun Tzu's The Art of War 2:2:1

"The best plan is to profit by the folly of others."
Pliny The Elder

General Principle: All key principles focus on making our average decisions profitable.

Situation:

Competition is uncertain and difficult. In competition, our resources are always limited. Running out of resources is fatal. We can know neither the costs nor benefits of a given move before we make it. Because of the uncertainties involved, we do know that every move will have costs and not all our moves will generate benefits. Many moves will consume more resources than they generate. We are taught in school

that events can be foreseen and actions planned, but the predictability of plans are very different in a controlled environment than in a competitive environment. This mindset that assumes that the profitability of our actions can be predicted exactly is not only wrong but it can be fatal.

Opportunity:

Sun Tzu's The Art of War was the first work to recognize that success is always based on relatively simple economics. In modern science, the concept of strategic profitability is known as Minimax Theory , which is used in decision theory , game theory , statistics , philosophy. The idea is minimizing the possible loss while maximizing the potential gain. From the perspective of the competitive strategist and, fortunately for us all, the Sun Tzu's minimax model is much simpler than the one used in traditional game theory. It requires no math. It requires mastering only a few key principles. We don't worry about calculating only about minimizing and maximizing. We compare probabilities. We worry about time.

Key Methods:

To make profitable decisions, each of the nine formulas of Sun Tzu's system are all based about a profit strategy:

1. Understand the difference between competition, battle, fighting, and conflict. These four terms are used interchangeably in casual conversation, but we require more precise definitions so we can understand what is necessary and what is not.

- *Competition* is a comparison of alternatives positions of opponents.
- *Battle* is a meeting of potential opponents where positions are compared.
- *F ighting* is expending resources to overcome a challenge.
- *Conflict* is the attempt to damage our opposition so we can take their position. Conflict is a meeting, i.e, battle, that requires resources, i.e, a fight, but it has the specific

goal of hurting opponents enough so that they will surrender a position to us.

2. All competition requires battles. Since all all competition is a comparison, such meetings are eventually necessary. By this definition, every buying decisions and sporting event is a battle, a situation where alternatives are compared. (1.3.1 Competitive Comparison)

3. B*oth advancing and defending our position requires various types of fights.* In other words, we must always use resources to overcome challenges. Battles are just one type of fight. There are many types of fights such as overcoming barriers in moving to a new position. Facing challenges and the use of resources are equally unavoidable (3.1.1 Resource Limitations).

4. All conflict is the result of a miscalculation. Conflict doesn't occur unless both parties think they can triumph. Opponent will always surrender or evade a battle rather than enter into costly conflict that they know that they will certainly lose. The problem is that, because of our limited information, we naturally over estimate our own advantages and underestimate those of our opponents. Conflict (2.1.1 Information Limits).

5. Conflict is always unnecessary. There are an infinite number of opportunities that exist as unfilled positions that others desire to be filled. Conflict results from the mistake of zero-sum thinking, that we can only advance our position by taking someone else's position away. The environment is continually creating new opportunities as new needs (3.2 Opportunity Creation).

6. Conflict always creates costs. The specific problem with our trying to damage opponents is that opponents must defend themselves. When two opponents fight each other, both are diminished by the effort, losing resources that could be better utilized by finding other ways to advance their position. Since both positions are damaged, creating opportunities for others outside of the battle. Since defending a position is always less expensive than attacking it, this is most costly way of trying to advance a position (1.1.2 Defending Positions).

Illustration:

Let us look at these key methods in terms of business conflict. In business, battling over customers is never profitable, even if we win them. Whenever two businesses get into, for example, a price war, we can predict that the most likely outcome is that both will end up losing profits. For decades a whole series of companies battled IBM for dominance in the mainframe computer industry. None of them were successful and their investors lost a staggering amount of money. Then a series of companies challenged Microsoft only to fail. Now the same thinking causes people to want to challenge Google directly in the search engine business.

Let us look at the specific battles of Microsoft and Apple over computers and MP3 players.

1. Understand the difference between competition, battle, fighting, and conflict. All businesses compete because their products are compared with other alternative uses of money. Apple and Microsoft will always compete.

2. All competition requires battles. A business battle occurs at every point of sale, when the customer makes a decisions to buy one product instead of another. The computer store is a battlefield.

3. B*oth advancing and defending our position requires various types of fights.* Businesses such as Microsoft and Apple fight by spending money on advertising, merchandising, product development, etc. These fights don't become conflict until one competitor starts attacking the other.

4. All conflict is the result of a miscalculation. Conflict only occurs when one company tries to take away another's customers by positioning their products as a direct replacement for the products of others. Recording artists compete with each other without conflict in selling their music, but Microsoft and Apple engage in conflict in their sales of computers and MP3 players.

5. Conflict is always unnecessary. Most customers of Microsoft and Apple but their different products for very different reasons, but rather than go after different customers, Microsoft and Apple choose to go after conflicting markets.

6. *Conflict always creates costs*. These battles have cost both companies but both are profitable that they think that they can afford the luxury.

3.1.3 Conflict Cost

Description: Sun Tzu's six key methods on the costly nature of resolving competitive comparisons by conflict.

"You must avoid disasters from armed conflict."
Sun Tzu's The Art of War 7:1:5

"We must work to resolve conflicts in a spirit of reconciliation and always keep in mind the interests of others. We cannot destroy our neighbors! We cannot ignore their interests! Doing so would ultimately cause us to suffer."
Dalai Lama

General Principle: The biggest and most certain source of costs in advancing a position is conflict.

Situation:

Conflict defines wars of attrition. In such wars, the party that sustains the least damage is the technical winner. The problem is that, according to the economics of strategy, both parties in a conflict are much more likely to be losers in the long-term. These Pyrrhic victories occur when winning the battle costs us our success over the longer term. These "victories" cost much more than any benefit that we can ever hope to win from them.

Opportunity:

We avoid conflict not out of altruism but for the pragmatic reason that that success is much more likely without it. Strategy is the economics of advancing our position and in that economics, conflict is simply too costly (3.1 Strategic Economics). When competition is properly understood, we can advance our position while avoiding all the costs of competition. Competition is always a comparison (1.3.1 Competitive Comparison). We do not have to damage our opponents in order to come out on top in that comparison. The ideal position is one that others do not want to attack and ideally want to join. Correctly understood competition embraces cooperation because allies support our position. Conflict, not competition, is the opposite of cooperation.

Key Methods:

Our strategy is to meet a potential opponents under the right conditions so that we can win battles and even fights without conflict. This means that we can win the competition, i.e. comparison, without having to damage our opponents to demonstrate our superiority.

1. Understand the difference between competition, battle, fighting, and conflict. These four terms are used interchangeably in casual conversation, but we require more precise definitions so we can understand what is necessary and what is not.

- *Competition* is a comparison of alternatives positions of opponents.
- *Battle* is a meeting of potential opponents where positions are compared.
- *F ighting* is expending resources to overcome a challenge.

- ***Conflict*** is the attempt to damage our opposition so we can take their position. Conflict is a meeting, i.e, battle, that requires resources, i.e, a fight, but it has the specific goal of hurting opponents enough so that they will surrender a position to us.

   2. All competition requires battles. Since all all competition is a comparison, such meetings are eventually necessary. By this definition, every buying decisions and sporting event is a battle, a situation where alternatives are compared. (1.3.1 Competitive Comparison)

   3. B*oth advancing and defending our position requires various types of fights.* In other words, we must always use resources to overcome challenges. Battles are just one type of fight. There are many types of fights such as overcoming barriers in moving to a new position. Facing challenges and the use of resources are equally unavoidable (3.1.1 Resource Limitations).

   4. All conflict is the result of a miscalculation. Conflict doesn't occur unless both parties think they can triumph. Opponent will always surrender or evade a battle rather than enter into costly conflict that they know that they will certainly lose. The problem is that, because of our limited information, we naturally over estimate our own advantages and underestimate those of our opponents. Conflict (2.1.1 Information Limits).

   5. Conflict is always unnecessary. There are an infinite number of opportunities that exist as unfilled positions that others desire to be filled. Conflict results from the mistake of zero-sum thinking, that we can only advance our position by taking someone else's position away. The environment is continually creating new opportunities as new needs (3.2 Opportunity Creation).

   6. Conflict always creates costs. The specific problem with our trying to damage opponents is that opponents must defend themselves. When two opponents fight each other, both are diminished by the effort, losing resources that could be better utilized by finding other ways to advance their position. Since both positions are damaged, creating opportunities for others outside of the battle. Since defending a position is always less expensive than attacking it, this is most costly way of trying to advance a position ([1.1.2 Defending Positions](#)).

Illustration:

Let us apply these nine key methods to the simple and common goal of making more money in a career to see how they change the nature of the challenge.

1. ***Our profit strategy starts by advancing our goals by finding more profitable positions.*** Instead of working harder or even smarter to get more money, look for ways to advance your position.

2. ***Our profit strategy relies on leveraging knowledge being less costly than using physical resources***. Learning more about the job market and employers is less costly than going to more interviews.

3. ***Our profit strategy utilizes "openings" to reduce the costs of advancing a position***. Find positions that are looking for applicants instead of positions that have more than they need.

4. ***Our profit strategy finds the openings most likely to produce profits based on our current position***. Look for positions that are connected to your current situation through people, skills, or intellectual topography.

5. ***Our profit strategy uses many small moves rather than a few large ones to reduce cost and risk.*** Do not look to find a perfect position but a position that allows you to gradually improve your position little-by-little.

6. ***Our profit strategy uses proven responses to increase the percentage of successful moves***. Know the common challenges you will face in getting promotions and be prepared with the right responses.

7. ***Our profit strategy creates momentum to reduce the costly friction in establishing a position***. Build up tension and use surprises to release it to break down the usual resistance to promotions.

8. ***Our profit strategy maximizes benefits by knowing the steps needed get the most rewards out of a move.*** Continually package and repackage the benefits that you offer others in expanding your ground.

9. ***Our profit strategy defends rewarding positions because defense is less expensive than offense.*** Always defend your current job situation before attempting to find a better one.

3.1.4 Openings

Description: Sun Tzu's seven key methods on seeking openings avoids costly conflict.

Advance where he can't defend.
Charge through his openings.
                    Sun Tzu's The Art of War 6:3:6-7

"A good deal happens in a man's life that he isn't responsible for. Fortunate openings occur; but it is safe to remember that such "breaks" are occurring all the time, and other things being equal, the advantage goes to the man who is ready."
                    Lawrence Downs

General Principle: Advance positions by using openings to avoid costly conflict.

Situation:

Competition seeks rewards. Rewards come from positions that control ground. Conflict is a mistake based on two misconceptions. The first is that there is only a finite amount of ground. The second is that existing ground can yield only a limited amount of rewards. If the ground and its resources are limited, conflict is unavoidable. As the number of people increase, they can only win rewards by taking from others. This would mean that the costs of conflict are also unavoidable and that all of humanity is locked into a war of attrition in which we all must grow poorer protecting what we have. Sun Tzu taught that this viewpoint was simply wrong.

Opportunity:

Sun Tzu taught that the ground as the stable source of rewards is infinite. He also taught that the climate as the changing source of opportunities is also infinite. Sun Tzu predicted that we would never run short of new, valuable ground. If he could see this truth from an agrarian culture 2,500 years ago, why do we still have problems seeing it today when the hottest real estate is the brand new terrain of the Internet? Sun Tzu recognized that the value of the ground came only from our knowledge about how to use it. As our knowledge grows, new resources become available from new types of ground. The only key resource is the human mind and its ability to learn.

Key Methods:

Conflict avoidance leads directly to the deeper lessons of strategy, especially a deeper understanding of the nature of positions and opportunities. Understood correctly, we can advance our positions in any direction. Once we stop focusing on what others have, there are undiscovered opportunities all around us. The wisest way to direct our energies is to look for rewards in areas where we have no opposition.

1. Opportunities exist as empty positions?openings?not positions that are already taken. We move into openings. We must especially avoid areas that are crowded with potential competitors. The conflict model of strategy focuses us on our perceived opponents instead of the larger environment where our opportunities lie. While we must be aware of our opponent's position in the environment, we use that awareness to help us identify where our opportunities might lie (1.3.1 Competitive Comparison).

2. *Openings exists both in physical space and the psychological landscape in people minds.* Positions always have both a physical and psychological dimension. When new physical ground is opened by discoveries, new psychological ground is always opened as well. Strategy works on both levels but it often focuses on the less visible psychological dimensions because its importance is easily missed (1.2 Subobjective Positions).

3. *The easiest way to find psychological openings is to look for unsatisfied needs*. Success means making victory pay and nothing pays better than satisfying people's needs. As we cannot say too often, a successful position is one that others cannot attack and ideally want to join. The power of looking for openings as needs is that it moves us away from conflict with others and into areas where we can win people's support (2.3 Personal Interactions).

4. *There are an infinite number of potential open positions in the environment.* The ground is unlimited because the knowledge that opens new ground is unlimited. Psychological ground is infinite because human needs are infinite. As soon as one need is filled, another one opens up. No matter how dominant our opponents are, they always leave plenty of openings for us to exploit. The future is not predictable because no one can know all the forms opportunity can take in the future (2.1.2 Leveraging Uncertainty

5. *Openings leverage the forces of the environment to work for us rather than against us*. Nature abhors a vacuum. By seeing opportunities as openings in the larger environment, we leverage the natural forces in the environment that are seeking to fill that opening. This is particularly easy when we are working on the psychological level of people's unfulfilled needs. People reward us to fill their needs (3.2.1 Environmental Dominance).

6. *Our discovery of new ground is limited only by our imagination.* Our creative ability is the source of discovery. Innovation creates new methods. New methods opens new ground. This is what Sun Tzu refers to as "surprise" in the quote. Creativity is not a rare skill, but a task that we can learn to do in a systematic way (7.3 Strategic Innovation).

7. Creatively using openings takes control from our opponents. When we fight over existing ground, we put our opponents in control of our situation. When we explore new ground, we take the initiative away from our opponents. The creative approach to opportunities puts us in control of our own position and situation. The more inventive we are in creating our own position, the less competition that we have. As we advance our position by exploring new ground, we gain greater and greater control over time. The idea that creativity creates momentum is one of the major principles of strategy (7.0 Creating Momentum).

Illustration:

This idea of openings exists in every competitive arena, but it is especially easy to see it in high-technological businesses since their very existence is based on it.

1. Opportunities exist as empty positions, i.e. openings, not positions that are already taken. It wasn't the companies that challenged IBM in the mainframe industry who became the new leaders in hi-tech. They all lost money. From Microsoft to Google, the winners are those who found open positions and developed them.

2. Openings exists both in physical space and the psychological landscape in people minds. When a new technological world like the Internet is opened up, our minds start immediately to populate it with the names of the companies and products. The map of the terrain isn't only the technological products themselves but how we place them in relationship to each other.

3. The easiest way to find psychological openings is to look for unsatisfied needs. As the Internet grew, searching it became the dominant need for users but advertising became the dominating need for providers. While others addressed each of these needs separately, Google brought them together.

4. *There are an infinite number of potential open positions in the environment.* Technology will open new areas like the Internet and new companies will arise to fill the needs in those areas.

5. *Openings leverage the forces of the environment to work for us rather than against us*. Companies such as Amazon and Ebay grow without even having to advertise because their users promote their products.

6. *Our discovery of new ground is limited only by our imagination.* We cannot even imagine the products of the future because the pioneers are so far ahead of us.

7. *Creatively using openings takes control from our opponents.* Apple's computers are doing better than ever but their success is driven by the iPod, a product that took Apple entirely away from the competitive fray.

3.1.5 Unpredictable Value

Description: Sun Tzu's seven key methods regarding the limitations of predicting the value of positions.

"Keep your army moving and plan for surprises."
Sun Tzu's The Art of War 11:3:8

"Greatness is a road leading towards the unknown."
Charles de Gaulle

General Principle: The cost and value of positions is unpredictable before exploration.

Situation:

Since strategy is the economics of advancing a position, moving into unoccupied and unexplored territory carries its own risk. When it comes to dealing with the unknown, there are two bad assumptions that we can make. Both lead to dangerous mistakes. First, we can think that because no one is currently occupying a position, there is no value to that position. This leads to conflict. The opposite mistake is to think that every open territory is valuable, some kind of gold mine. This leads to another costly mistake: our waste of limited resources.

Opportunity:

We avoid these mistakes by avoiding assumptions. We accept our ignorance about new territory (2.1.1 Information Limits). We avoid conflict and waste by refusing to make assumptions about the costs or potential value of a given opening. Imagination is a wonderful thing but it is a double-edged sword. While it requires imagination to see our opportunities, we have to be careful not to imagine what we cannot know: the potential profitability of a new position. We cannot advance our position without faith and optimism, but, since we are exploring new territory, we must balance our faith and optimism with methods that avoid disaster (5.0 Minimizing Mistakes).

Key Methods:

Opportunities represent the *potential* for rewards, but what do we know for certain about openings? We must understand the natural limits of the potential profitability of a move before we make it.

1. We know that openings offer no apparent direct opposition. This means that they are potentially less costly to explore than moving against occupied positions. This could be a relative advantage, but, while *seeming* empty, these positions may not actually *be* empty. As we move into them, others can be drawn to them as well. This fact forms the basis of a very common strategic situation (6.4.3 Contentious Situations).

2. Knowing that an opening exists doesn't tell us anything of its value. Open ground is not necessarily valuable ground. When we move to unoccupied positions, we must admit that we know nothing about either the cost of exploring those positions or their potential value. We know that exploring openings is less expensive than conflict, but lower costs do not mean making profit. To make a profit, the position must produce value. We cannot know that. This uncertainty is the main reason that people make the mistake of pursuing occupied positions. We know what those positions are worth. Their value has already been proven (3.1.2 Strategic Profitability).

3. ***We cannot extrapolate from the known into the unknown.*** Unexplored positions will be similar to nearby positions in some ways and different in other ways. The problem is that we cannot know in which ways they will be similar and in which ways they will be different. Our fears project the worst into the unknown while our hopes project the best but neither brings us nearer the truth (2.1.1 Information Limits).

4. ***Knowing probabilities is not the same as knowing actualities***. We can know what areas are *likely* to have relatively lower costs and high rewards but this doesn't tell us the real value of any opportunity. We must make decisions about where to explore based on these probabilities but even the highest probability gamble is still a gamble. Those who treat a gamble as if it was a sure thing are soon out of the game (4.0 Leveraging Probability).

5. ***We have to go to a place to know a place.*** Absence is the ultimate barrier to knowledge. We only get solid information about the cost and value of positions by exploring them. Since by definition no one is occupying an empty position, we cannot get information about it from anyone else. Until we make the trip, we are savages looking up at the moon and guessing what it might be like. This is why it is always necessary to make a move (5.6.2 Acting Now).

6. ***The only value we are assured is that of more information***. The goal is experimentation and exploration. The competitive world is a maze and many of its branches are dead-ends. When we explore a dead end, we get a little better picture of our situation. We want to make as few wrong turns as possible but when we make a wrong turn, we must learn from it. Each piece of the puzzle helps us put together the big picture (2.5 The Big Picture).

7. ***We cannot deem exploration a mistake on the basis of knowledge gained from it***. Even though many of our explorations will prove to be fruitless, we can only get that information from making the journey.

Illustration:

We are going to illustrate these principles with a discussion about the value of the Iraq war in terms of costs and benefits. Though this illustration may prove to be controversial, it is an extremely good example of economic unpredictability.

1. We know that openings offer no apparent direct opposition. It was assumed that after the mission was accomplished in deposing Saddam, that Iraq would be an open for the creation of a Arab democracy, but that opening attracted opposition that raised the costs dramatically.

2. Knowing that an opening exists doesn't tell us anything of its real value. Even though the costs of the opposition are largely behind us, we still do not know if the democracy in Iraq is yielding any benefits. There appears to be a movement toward democracy in the region, but even the future of Iraq in that regard is uncertain.

3. We cannot extrapolate from the known into the unknown. Iraq is different than building democracies in post-war Europe or Japan, but we cannot yet know how it is different.

4. Knowing probabilities is not the same as knowing actualities. We knew that Saddam probably had weapons of mass destruction because he had had them in the past, but we did not know anything about the real nature of his capabilities at the time of the invasion. We especially did not know about the nuclear proliferation program out of Pakistan that was active not only in Iraq, but Syria, Libya, and Iran.

5. We have to go to a place to know a place. We turned over a rock and instead of finding the expected scorpion of chemical and biological weapons we found a much more deadly snake nest of Pakistani nuclear proliferation.

6. The only value we are assured is that of more information. Knowledge helps, but it is what we do with it that matters. Knowing about the nuclear proliferation helped put an end to it in Libya and Syria, but Iran still hasn't been dealt with.

7. *We cannot deem exploration a mistake on the basis of knowledge gained from it*. To attack the war in Iraq because we didn't find the ***expected*** weapons of mass destruction makes no sense because we couldn't have know what weapons were there without the war itself. We cannot criticize our ignorance by saying that that ignorance didn't justify the actions that were the only possible way of ending that same ignorance.

3.1.6 Time Limitations

Description: Sun Tzu nine key methods for understanding the time limits on opportunities.

"Each day passes quickly.
A month can decide your failure or success."
Sun Tzu's The Art of War 6:8:15

""Four things come not back: the spoken word, the sped arrow, the past life and the neglected opportunity."
Arabian Proverb

General Principle: The time limitations of opportunities depend on economics.

Situation:

People inherently realize that all opportunities are temporary. We talk about "windows of opportunity" opening up and then closing. Because only our environment creates opportunities and is always changing, the temporary nature of opportunities is unavoidable. However, these basic ideas tell us very little about how to recognize whether an opportunity is waxing or waning.

Opportunity:

The temporary nature of opportunities evolves from economics (3.1 Strategic Economics). There is an economic life cycle in which opportunities emerge, mature, and eventually disappear. We define nine stages in this life-cycle that follow the nine stages of a campaign (6.4 Nine Situations). Once we master these stages, we can pretty quickly get a fix on where a given opportunity is in its evolution and what the best strategy is for exploring it (6.3 Campaign Patterns).

Key Methods:

The cycle of an opportunity starts in ignorance. In the beginning, people can know neither the location of an opportunity nor if it is valuable nor the method for exploiting it nor the size of the opportunity. As the opportunity is explored, all four of these areas--location, value, methods, and size--are resolved through the economic life cycle. In the beginning of this cycle, the opening is the greatest but the rewards are the least certain since so much is unknown. However, those who get into this cycle at the earlier stages always have a first mover advantage over those who come later. The ability to survive one stage and make it to the next depends upon understanding what each situation requires.

1. The climate changes, creating new open ground, but no one sees it. This is the first stage during which location of the opportunity is unknown. People fight over what they can see instead of going into the new area that is as yet invisible (3.2.2 Opportunity Invisibility).

2. A few innovators see the opportunity and start exploring it. At this stage, these early explorers don't know whether or not the ground is valuable. Early exploration simply looks for value. This is the easiest stage because few competitors are involved and the opportunity is still wide open (6.4.2 Easy Situations).

3. ***The ground proves valuable and more are drawn to it.*** If an opening does not prove valuable, it is no longer an opportunity. If early explorations do discover value, others will find out about it and be drawn to the opportunity. The increase of people exploring the ground increases the potential for conflict even though the method and size of the ground are not yet know (6.4.3 Contentious Situations).

4. ***Different people explore different methods to make the new ground rewarding.*** This is the stage in which people begin to explore different methods for getting rewards out of an opportunity. At this stage, no one knows the best method or even if there is any one best method. They look for different paths for controlling the ground but keep an eye on what others are doing in the area, trying to keep pace with them (6.4.4 Open Situations).

5. ***A single best method emerges and people compete for control.*** At this stage, location, value, and methods of the ground have been proven. The remaining issue is the size of the opportunity and how many people will share in controlling it. Competitors now look to put together dominating positions in competition with each other. This is the end of the opportunity for those who are not already in contention (6.4.5 Intersecting Situations).

6. ***Economics begins to squeeze out competitors.*** At this stage, those exploring an opportunity must become self-funded from within the opportunity itself. Outside funding for exploration dries up as the leaders emerge in the previous stage. Those who remain are those who are supporting themselves from their positions within the new area of opportunity (6.4.6 Serious Situations).

7. ***The size limits of the opportunity are reached.*** Some ground never reaches this stage because new areas off of it keep opening up, but most areas have limits. This stage marks another point at which the opportunity is fading. At this stage, a few dominate players have positions controlling all the valuable ground. The situation shifts from a true opportunity to a local zero-sum game. This is the end of the growth phase and the beginning of a contraction phase. Competitive skills begin to become less important than production skills (6.4.7 Difficult Situations).

8. *The climate begins to shift, and profitability diminishes*. At this stage, the opportunity reaches a point of diminishing returns. In the previous phase, conflict became more likely, but now it becomes a matter for survival. As the size of the competitive area itself begins to shrink in an absolute sense with the changes in climate, competitors are forced into conflict, destroying the profitability of the ground (6.4.8 Limited Situations).

9. *The ground is no longer profitable*. This is the final stage. It is reached when the cost of maintaining a position on the ground outweighs its value. If this point is reached, the ground must be abandoned. Those occupying it are forced to find new positions elsewhere. The ground is returned to its original empty state (6.4.9 Desperate Situations).

Illustration:

Let us follow this life cycle through a technology that has come and gone, that of traditional "mainframe" computers for data-processing.

1. *The climate changes, creating new open ground, but no one sees it*. This is the era of mechanical machines that are limited to doing mechanical mathematical calculations but not data processing. IBM was a maker of such mechanical adding machines.

2. *A few innovators see the opportunity and start exploring it*. The work in WWII on early computers makes it appear that something is practical but IBM says the market is limited to perhaps six such machines in the world.

3. *The ground proves valuable and more are drawn to it*. More than six machines are sold and more and more companies are drawn to the market as more and more people see its potential. ***Different people explore different methods to make the new ground rewarding.*** Many different types of architectures and designs are tried as issues regarding memory, storage, and programming are addressed.

4. A single ***best method emerges and people compete for control.*** Standard architectures and languages emerge. Companies begin to vie for dominance with IBM coming out on top. ***Economics begins to squeeze out competitors***. Companies that invested large amounts in trying to establish a mainframe business such as Sperry Rand with Univac cannot make it pay and begin to drop out in the 50s.

5. ***The size limits of the opportunity are reached.*** While the limits of computing were not reached, the limits of mainframe architecture were. Because of their cost, only certain organizations were able to support them. IBM and two or three other companies control the market.

6. ***The climate begins to shift, and profitability diminishes***. Mainframes started to be replaced first by minicomputers and then networks of servers. The cost of building and supporting the traditional architecture, operating systems, and languages begins to outweigh their value.

7. ***The ground is no longer profitable***. The traditional mainframe fades away and IBM becomes primarily a service company.

3.2 Opportunity Creation

Description: Five key methods regarding how change creates opportunities.

"Know when the terrain is open."
Sun Tzu's The Art of War 11:1:5

"There exist limitless opportunities in every industry. Where there is an open mind, there will always be a frontier."

Charles Kettering

General Principle: Opportunities are created by the natural forces of desire.

Situation:

Our world consists of 6 billion people constantly shifting through a rapidly changing kaleidoscope of actions, encounters, plans, and desires. Each competitive arena plays a part in this turbulent dance and cannot be separated from it. Larger and tiny opportunities are constantly arising and disappearing in this rich bubbling stew, but predicting where these opportunities will arise and where they will go seems impossible. This turbulence of change is both frightening and enticing. It threatens our current position at the same time it offers the possibility of improving it. We want to ride these changes, but they are always different, their paths seem random, and our encounters with them largely a matter of chance.

Opportunity:

Opportunity is created by two opposing natural processes. On one side, nature abhors a vacuum. On the other, dynamic environments continually create openings (3.1.4 Openings). We leverage nature's "desire" to fill openings by advancing our position into these openings. These forces continually degrade existing positions while continually creating new opportunities. Joseph Schumpeter called this process "creative destruction" (1.8.1 Creation and Destruction). The more dynamic the environment, the more opportunities it creates, but the shorter the life-span of any existing position.

Key Methods:

Nature's desire to fill a vacuum is echoed in our human desires. While we can occasionally leverage physical open spaces, we usually use the openings of need and desire. We all have unfulfilled desires. As one desire is met, another desire takes its place. While we can complain about this "greed," it is an unchanging force of nature. Even those who are quick to criticize the selfish desires of others do so because they desire to control others based on a "common good" that only reflects their selfish desires.

We need a powerful set of mental models to help us understand this complex interplay of often conflicting desires. It is the general key methods of change driven by complementary opposites and the specific principles of opportunity.

1. Only *the environment creates the openings of opportunity.* Nature gives us certain resources but creates the need in us for

other resources. Trying to create our own opportunities is a waste of our effort because they come from within other people. We do not create the needs of others any more than we create our own needs. We cannot advance our position unless others support us. People do not support us unless they desire to do so. We are only rewarded for satisfying the needs of others (3.2.1 Environmental Dominance).

2. Opportunities are difficult to see because they are empty. We can see exchanges, when people are rewarded for satisfying needs, but new opportunities that no one is satisfying is nearly impossible to see. Emptiness is invisible. There are small openings all around us, but we usually cannot see them because we are too occupied with our own larger desires to notice the minor desires of others around us (3.2.2 Opportunity Invisibility).

3. Opportunity exists in the potential of balancing of opposites. This balance is easier to see as an exchange of resources. We trade what we have in abundance for what we lack. This is how value is created: a surplus in one place is exchanged for a different surplus somewhere else in the environment. This exchange is motivated solely by need but is possible because people have different needs and different resources that complement each other. Value is created by putting these complementary resources where they are the *most* needed. Our positions enable these exchanges of complementary opposites (3.2.2 Complementary Opposites).

4. All opportunities can be described in terms of emptiness and fullness. There are a million different forms of need. Each need requires different resources, but the general principle is that desire and resources are always balancing. Emptiness describes any state of need or lack of resources. Fullness is its opposite, a state of satiety and a surplus of resources. Both states are temporary, where one must give way to the other over time, creating one another in a constant cycle. The advantage in seeing the world as a cycle of emptiness and fullness is that it simplifies that kaleidoscope of different needs into just two possible states (3.2.3 Emptiness and Fullness).

5. Abundance suddenly reverses into new forms of need. New needs emerge not from an accumulation of older needs but from the satisfaction of need. Abundance arises because we improve the exchanges that move resources to where they are needed. This abundance provides the resources for addressing existing needs, but in doing so, always creates new types of needs, often spilling over into entirely unforeseen areas of desire. Another way of saying this is that desire is an emergent property of abundance (3.2.5 Dynamic Reversal).

Illustration:

Let us consider how the opportunity for manufacturing, selling, and using MP3 players was created.

1. Only the environment creates opportunity because need arises from nature. If the enjoyment of music was not born within us, the MP3 player would not exist. If we didn't desire more music in more places at more times, we wouldn't want MP3 players.

2. Opportunities are difficult to see because they are empty. The advantages of music in a digital form instead of a physical form was difficult for people to understand until they were exposed to it over time and is still very difficult for the music industry.

3. Opportunity exists in the potential of balancing of opposites. Thousand of resources must be exchanged to provide the resources necessary to create an MP3 player. All of those resources have value because people value music and are willing to exchange the value that they create for the MP3 player to have it.

4. All opportunities can be described in terms of emptiness and fullness. Music is a form of fullness satisfying the emptiness that is the desire for music.

5. Abundance suddenly reverses into new forms of need. The abundance of smart MP3 players has created the need for more portable application beyond just music.

3.2.1 Environmental Dominance

Description: Sun Tzu's five key methods on why openings must be created by others.

"Your war can take any shape.
It must avoid the strong and strike the weak.
Water follows the shape of the land that directs its flow.
Your forces follow the enemy who determines how you
win."

Sun Tzu's The Art of War 6:8:4-8

"Ability is of little account without opportunity."

Napoleon Bonaparte

General Principle: The competitive environment creates all our opportunities for us.

Situation:

If we think we can create our own opportunities, we are wrong. Within our span of control , we can always improve ourselves and our operations in terms of efficiency and effectiveness. The problem is that these improvements may or may not have any affect upon our external position, which is realm of opportunity. Only external conditions make our internal improvements valuable to others. The problem is that we do not create or control these conditions in our competitive environment. We especially cannot control the "openings" in the environment that represent opportunities. Whether we think about these openings as open spaces or as unfulfilled psychological needs, efforts to create opportunities always waste resources. They are driven by the illusion of control.

Opportunity:

Sun Tzu's strategy leverages the forces within the environment. For better or worse, we are moved forward by events and conditions like a sailing ship is moved by the wind. We cannot control these condition, but we can know how to use them. We control our progress and direction in the same way a sailing ship does, by knowing how to use these forces. We take the actions that work these forces in our advantage. In Sun Tzu's system, "an advantage" means a position that is favored by the forces in the environment over alternative positions. An opportunity is an opening that allows us to move into a position that has more advantages that our current position.

Key Methods:

1. We cannot create opportunities from our own skills and efforts alone. A need for our skills must exist in the environment and we must know where and how to find and use that opening. An opportunity is an opening, an empty space. We do not create that space. The decisions of others that leave that space open. In psychological space, we do not create the needs that others feel. We also do not create the situation by which that need is left unsatisfied. We take advantage of openings, but we do not create them (3.1.4 Openings).

2. The environment makes the rules that define opportunity. We can't fool Mother Nature. Every battleground has its own rules and those rule arise from the nature of the environment. We don't make these rules. Even in a sports contest the most important rules, the laws of physics, are not made or enforced by officials. Some are straight forward and obvious, such as the law of gravity. Others arise as emergent properties of complex systems, unforeseen and unpredictable. We not only don't make these rules, we can never completely understand them. Despite all our progress, we describe most of the universe as "dark matter" and "dark energy" to express our vast ignorance (1.4 The External Environment).

3. The forces creating opportunities are larger than they seem. Opportunity creation involves interactions between all parts of our environment. Our local situation is not separated from this larger whole but intimately connected to it though our knowledge of those connections is extremely limited (2.1.1 Information Limits). The amount of force required to open up opportunities in this vast network to depends on the size and duration of the opening, but the force required to make any change is larger than it appears. A trick of perspective can make us seem more relatively powerful than we are. What is closer to us appears larger than what is distant, confusing us about our relative influence to form our external environment on our own (1.2 Subobjective Positions).

4. Nature makes us overconfident about our ability to control. We need confidence to see and act on opportunities around us, but Sun Tzu teaches confidence is as dangerous in excess as it is in absence. In psychology and economics, this problem is known as overconfidence bias. All the research demonstrates the we systematically are overconfident about the likely success of our plans, discounting the effect of factors outside of our control (4.7.1 Command Weaknesses).

5. *Opportunity cannot exist without external rewards.* Competitive goals always include reward from the outside. Advancing positions also means gaining control of more resources and these resources must exist in the environment. We don't put them there ourselves. We cannot advance our position unless others support us. People do not support us unless we help them meet their needs. We are only rewarded for satisfying the needs of others. The size and complexity of the competitive environment makes its potential in terms of hidden resources impossible to know (3.1.1 Resource Limitations).

Illustration:

Let us simply look at the opportunity to start your own business.

1. We cannot create opportunities from our own skills and efforts alone. If we are good at doing our job, we are tempted to think we can start our own business to do it. Let us look specifically at the problem of a good cooks, that thinks that he or she can open new restaurant on the basis of their skill alone. We pick this example because many people, including many professional chefs, think that because they know their skill, they can create an opportunity for themselves.

2. The environment makes the rules that define opportunity. Even if we know the rules for making good food, we still have all the other rules for opening and running a successful restaurant. This includes everything from good restaurant design to the laws of economics. Many of these rules are non-intuitive, including the rules that openings for restaurants exist near other different types of restaurants.

3. The forces creating opportunities are larger than they seem. With modern travel, today's diners have more dining options and broader experience than ever before. The most difficult challenge in running a restaurant is drawing diners to it to try it for the first time but diners have too many choices, they cannot try them all. Advertising is an extremely expensive way to do this, so restaurants open near other restaurants to take advantage of existing flows of diners.

They can be seen by those who dine out by choosing the right location.

4. Nature makes us overconfident about our ability to control. Chefs, like all people in the "arts" almost always over estimate the quality of their product from the perspective of others. They expect the tastiness of their cooking to create "word of mouth" in influencing others to try it. This effect is almost always smaller than anticipated. There is a lot of good food. People eat out a lot. Even good food doesn't make as much of an impression on diners as a chef will assume.

5. Opportunity cannot exist without external rewards. Chefs, like many who consider themselves artists, work to satisfy themselves rather than their customers. The result is that 80% of new restaurants go out business within the first few years as their savings slowly run out.

3.2.2 Opportunity Invisibility

Description: Sun Tzu five key methods on why opportunities are always hidden.

"You can never see all the shades of victory."
Sun Tzu's The Art of War 5:2:16

"To see what is in front of one's nose needs a constant struggle."
George Orwell

"Opportunity is often difficult to recognize; we usually expect it to beckon us with beepers and billboards."
William Arthur Ward

General Principle: Opportunities are hidden, and, once discovered, are no longer opportunities.

Situation:

Opportunities are like phantoms that we can only glimpse out of the corners of our eyes. When we look for them directly, they disappear. We want to see patterns that make the future predictable, but the future is not predictable. We only know one thing about the future for certain. It will be different from the past. Making this problem worse, we often see patterns that do not exist. In psychology, seeing patterns that do not exist is known as the clustering illusion. Our desire to see opportunities can lead to conflict. Another problem is the bandwagon effect , our tendency to follow the crowd. This leads us to see opportunities where others have already had success. The problem is that an opportunity that someone else has already used is no longer an opportunity at all.

Opportunity:

Seeing opportunities is a special skill that we must be trained to master. We cannot see them by looking at them directly. Like black holes, we can only infer their existence from the effects they create around them. Seeing opportunities is an act of imagination, and, done correctly, prevents us from charging after expired opportunities that others have already used up. The mental models taught by Sun Tzu require knowing our limits so we can work within them (2.2.2 Mental Models).

Key Methods:

The key methods relating to the invisibility of opportunities sets the boundary conditions for seeing opportunities.

1. The nature of opportunities as openings makes them difficult to see. Opportunities are openings. They are empty spaces and unmet needs. How do we see emptiness? What is it that we are looking for when we try to see an opportunity? There is literally nothing there. We cannot see the opportunity directly because it is literally nothing (3.1.4 Openings).

2. *Seeing an opportunity is an act of imagination.* What we see is an empty place in the puzzle. We then have to imagine the shape and color of the piece that fills that emptiness. Sometimes we are right. Often we are wrong. We don't know if anything really fills that hole until something clicks when we try to fill it (7.3.3 Creative Innovation).

3. *People only see expired opportunities, other people's opportunities.* They are not thinking about imagination. Instead, they are thinking about imitation. They see a situation that was once an opportunity and think that they can take advantage of it by duplicating the success of others. These people can see opportunities only once they have been filled with something. In other words, they only see situations when they are no longer opportunities but other people's successes (3.1.6 Time Limitations).

4. *Once identified, it is impossible to know the extent of an opportunity.* Some opportunity doesn't mean enough opportunity to reward us for our efforts. We can know only one thing about the potential size of an opportunity at the beginning. We will only know its extent when when it begins to run out. It grows and grows until it reaches it limits. When it reaches those limits, that growth stops, sometimes quite suddenly. We can only guess at size until the excavation is done 3.1.1 Resource Limitations).

5. *Opportunities exist only in the future and the future is invisible*. We cannot know the future. Future potential of shifting climate is just one part of this problem. Thinking that we can know the future is what is known as hindsight bias. The past looks as though it was predictable when it wasn't. Some of the cycles of climate are predictable, but innovation is also part of the future and it changes patterns of potential. We never know when the next creative bolt of insight is going to strike, suddenly opening up new competitive landscapes and changing our situation forever (7.3 Strategic Innovation).

Illustration:

Since we recently saw the collapse of the housing bubble that so many saw as an opportunity, let us use that as an example of the dangers here. Was buying a house at that point in time an opportunity?

1. The nature of opportunities as openings makes them difficult to see. House prices go up 300% in a short period of time. A lot of people have made money flipping houses. Mortgage requirements and interest rates are at record lows. In the last, more dangerous years of the bubble, everyone saw the opportunity. That alone should have been the clue that the opportunity was gone.

2. Seeing an opportunity is an act of imagination. It took no imagination to see the value of housing and how it had increased. The real opportunity in housing existed before houses went up 300%, but who could see the opportunity then? Prices were stable. Interest rates were high. Financing hurdles were significant. Nobody was making money.

3. People only see expired opportunities, other people's opportunities. There was an opportunity, but it was gone. What was left was not an opportunity. As too many people have discovered, it was more of a trap than an opportunity as they bought houses that were soon worth less than their mortgages.

4. Once identified, it is impossible to know the extent of an opportunity. When did the opportunity end? The answer was different in different places, but the only important answer is that the extent of the opportunity was impossible to know before the bubble burst.

5. Opportunities exist only in the future and the future is invisible. Now everyone says that it was obvious that the housing market was oversold, but it wasn't.

3.2.3 Complementary Opposites

Description: Sun Tzu five key methods regarding the dynamics of balance from opposing forces.

"Know the enemy and know yourself. Your victory will be painless.
Know the climate and the ground.
Your victory will be complete."

Sun Tzu's The Art of War 10:5:15-18

"The opposite of a correct statement is a false statement. But the opposite of a profound truth may well be another profound truth."

Niels Bohr

General Principle: Look for new opportunities in a balancing of opposites.

Situation:

We are trained in linear thinking , which leads to "straight line" predictions. When a trend continues in one direction for a period of time, we naturally begin to think that it will always continue in that direction. The problem is that in the real world, we more commonly see a regression toward the mean , a return to balance. In the West, we have a deterministic and reductionist view of systems, but Plato was the first to recognize that these linear methods have natural limits. Sun Tzu based his system for discovering opportunities on the Chinese philosophy of yin-yang.

Opportunity:

While we cannot predict the future exactly, looking for the balancing forces dramatically improves our ability to find opportunities (1.4.1 Climate Shift). The future does not flow in a straight line, but in an undulating cycle arising from the contest between opposing forces. Many forms of opportunities can be found in positioning ourselves to take advantage of the reversing of these cycles. As our herd instinct takes most people in one direction, openings arise in the opposite direction. These cycles swing between opposite extremes that are the heart of Sun Tzu's system. When conditions swing too far in one direction, it is highly probably that they will start back in the opposite direction.

Key Methods:

There are a great many balancing forces that affect competitive advantage. In Sun Tzu's strategy, we call these balancing forces complementary opposites. Using Sun Tzu's methods we find opportunities in predictable cycles. These cycles repeat themselves in similar ways. This is because they are driven by complementary opposites, where the extremes are known and the balancing forces are understood at least to some degree.

1. All natural systems consist of a balance of opposing forces called complementary opposites. If nature didn't consist of a balance of forces, the universe wouldn't exist. All strategic conditions reflect the waxing and waning of these opposing forces. These underlying forces cannot always be known, but they are always there. Sun Tzu's strategy identifies dozens of complementary opposites that come into play in specific situations. Even the most basic elements of a strategic--ground and climate, command and methods--are defined as complementary opposites (1.3 Elemental Analysis).

2. *No trend continues forever because its extension naturally exhausts the force of the dominant opposite.* A trend in one direction is driven by the currently dominant half of a complementary pair. Over time, it requires more and more resources to drive the trend forward. All resources are limited, even those of natural forces. Eventually resources of the dominant half are stretched too thinly and the trend begins to reverse as the other half grows relatively stronger. We don't know what those limits are before we reach them, but their limitations are certain (3.1.1 Resource Limitations).

3. *The stronger the trend, the shorter the life span of the opposing force*. Gradual trends last longer than dramatic trends simply because resources of the dominant half are expended more quickly. Accelerating trends do not necessarily decelerate before they reverse themselves. Resources can suddenly reach their limit. This often leads to sudden crashes of the most dramatic trends (1.1.1 Position Dynamics).

4. *Opportunities are created at the extremes of shifts between complementary opposites.* Because most people make straight line predictions, the greatest number of people expect the dominant trend to continue at those extremes. This creates an opening. Few are prepared for that trend to reverse itself. Our opportunity is positioning ourselves so that the rising force of the other half of the balance carries us with it, harnessing the force of nature to advance our position (4.0 Leveraging Probability).

5. *The growth of human knowledge is outside the natural balance of forces*. Human progress is possible because knowledge stands apart from the balancing forces of nature. It is our understanding about those natural forces and how to leverage them. Each new type of knowledge or technology has its limits, but the extension of our knowledge itself can go on indefinitely. The end of one cycle in learning, opens up the potential of a new cycle of learning in a new direction. This makes the direction of these cycles of innovation beyond the time-line of S-curve itself impossible to predict (7.5.2 The Spread of Innovation).

6. Complex systems isolate us from the underlying balance of forces on which they are based. This is the one sense in which our knowledge creates its balancing force of ignorance. We embody our growing knowledge in systems. As our systems grow in complexity, we lose track of the natural forces on which they are based. We live in the artificial world that we have created. In this artificial world, we develop new mental models based on artifice instead of reality. Utopian systems of perfect control and predictability only seem possible because we are cut off from the underlying balance of forces on which our world is based (2.1.1 Information Limits).

Illustration:

There are all types of complementary opposites, but we can't cover them all. Since we are interested specifically in making progress, let us look specifically at technological growth.

1. **All natural systems consist of a balance of opposing forces called complementary opposites.** The positive and negative electrical charges, the opposite sexes, the economic cycles of greed and fear, our left and right hands are all different natural demonstrations of this rule.

2. **No trend continues forever because its extension naturally exhausts the force of the dominant opposite.** In the strategy of stock picking, this principle is called contrarian investing. In statistical analysis, it is reflected in the idea called "regression to the mean." When automobile and airplane technology is advancing as dramatically as they did in the 30s, we predicted rocket cars. We didn't get rocket cars because the physics of flight and economics of the assembly line have natural limits. When housing prices go up for a few decades, we start thinking that they will always go up. When the climate gets cooler or warming for a few decades, we

think that trend means the doom of civilization (see this post for a good chart showing a IPCCs straight line projection against real historical trends of heating and cooling). As computer technology improves dramatically, we start predicting " technological singularity " of limitless artificial intelligence.

3. The stronger the trend, the shorter the life span of the opposing force. The housing boom and the.com trends were dramatic, but each lasted less than a decade. The gradual improvements in breeding agricultural crops, in contrast, have continued for hundreds of years. The gradual increase in the value of gold has continued since currency was disconnected from the gold standard and will continue as long as governments can create money at will.

4. Opportunities are created at the extremes of shifts between complementary opposites. As the boom accelerates, sell the house as the boom trend accelerates. Buy houses as foreclosures increase. Though not technically a.com, I sold my software company in late 1997, before the software down slide that started in 1999.

5. The growth of human knowledge is outside the natural balance of forces. Never bet against human progress over the long-term. People will continue to learn and find methods that work better than older methods.

6. Complex systems isolate us from the underlying balance of forces on which they are based. In the middle of a boom, no one sees its underlying natural constraints. As money is printed, its value seems to hold for awhile but like a rubber band that is stretched and stretched, something eventually snaps. Money's artificial nature must pay homage eventually to underlying stores of natural value. Thus the rise of gold prices.

3.2.4 Emptiness and Fullness

Description: Sun Tzu's nine key methods on the transformations between emptiness and fullness.

"Avoid full and yet strike empty."
Sun Tzu's The Art of War 6:8:5 (Chinese Revealed).

"Strength is just an accident arising from the weakness of others."

Joseph Conrad

General Principle: Success in comparison arises naturally from focusing the fullness of strength on the emptiness of weakness.

Situation:

The saying is that opportunity never knocks twice, but opportunity is always knocking. The problem is that opportunity never repeats itself in the same way. All opportunities are unique in time and place. Another's opportunity is never exactly the same as our own. This makes identifying opportunities a challenge. Reality is too complicated for us to identify and analyze every possible condition that might represent an opportunity. Sun Tzu's strategy identifies many common opportunities indicators but he understood that such a list could never be complete. Opportunities are often based on the most unique aspects of the situation.

Opportunity:

Sun Tzu provides a simple mental model for searching for opportunities in a wide variety of unique situations. Our opportunities always arise in the transition back and forth between emptiness and fullness. We simplify our search for opportunities by changing our minds to think of everything in terms of emptiness and fullness. Emptiness is any lack, or vacuum, most commonly a human need or desire. Sadness, insignificance, hunger, slowness, and ignorance are types of emptiness. Fullness is whatever fills that lack, that vacuum, satisfying a particular need or desire. Happiness, significance, satiation, speed, and knowledge are forms of fullness. Happiness fills sadness. Satiation fulfills hunger. Knowledge fills up ignorance, and so on.

Key Methods:

Sun Tzu's concepts of emptiness and fullness are built on more basic key methods but extend beyond them.

1. We must avoid the full and seek the empty. All opportunities must be openings, positions that others have not occupied. By moving into openings, we avoid costly conflict (3.1.4 Openings).

2. Emptiness and fullness can take may different forms. Emptiness is any state of need or desire. Fullness is its opposite, a state of satiety and surplus. The advantage in seeing the world as cycles of emptiness and fullness is that it simplifies that kaleidoscope of different needs into just two possible states (3.2.3 Complementary Opposites).

3. Opportunity arises from the eternal shift among different forms of emptiness and fullness. Both states are temporary, where one must give way to the other over time, creating one another in a constant cycle. This cycle is endless. As one human need or desire is filled, another automatically arises. Needs that were once filled become empty again over time. We can use these constant shifts to our advantage (3.2 Opportunity Creation).

4. The shift among emptiness and fullness cannot be exactly predicted. When one need is filled, we do not know what new desire will take its place. We often cannot predict this for ourselves, much less others. The interplay among human priorities is inherently complex beyond human comprehension. Our opportunities exist at the juncture of what we have failed to foresee and others have also overlooked. People only need what they are not getting. We must see the opportunity, we cannot predict it (5.2 Opportunity Exploration).

5. Emptiness becomes our opportunity when we can fill it for others. The only forms of emptiness that create opportunities for us personally are those that we are in a position to fill for others. Emptiness is only an opportunity if it exists outside of ourselves, in others. Others will feel that emptiness in a way that we do not. This is why listening is the first step in the adaptive loop of listen>aim>move>claim. The openings that interest us as those that we can reach from our own position and fill using our internal resources of character and skill (1.5 Internal Elements).

6. Emptiness is a temporary state so opportunity requires speed. Emptiness is naturally balanced by nature. Depending on the type of need involved, the emptiness is either replaced by a greater need or grows until it must be addressed. Emptiness opens up and closes constantly. However, different types of emptiness reoccur in a pattern: the need to breath, the need to drink, the need to eat, and so on. We cannot aim at a specific opening for a specific person at a specific type because this cycle is based on probabilities not certainties, but the goal of strategy is to position ourselves for a certain type of emptiness. We want to be in the right time at the right place when that opening appears (1.6.3 Shifting Priorities).

7. Small empty spaces are much more common than large. Opportunity consist mostly of small, immediate forms of emptiness in the general direction that we want to move. These small openings are all around us, but we usually cannot see them because they are small and we are too occupied with our own larger desires to notice the minor needs of others around us. Often we can see them more easily if we focus on our own small needs because we often share them with others (3.2.2 Opportunity Invisibility).

8. *Small openings lead to larger ones.* Large openings that fit our skills are much less common than a smaller one, but are rare. In taking advantage of small openings. We undertake campaigns in order to gradually shift to better and better positions over time, making new, currently distant, resources attainable (1.8 Progress Cycle).

9. *One form of emptiness can require other different forms of fullness*. The concepts of emptiness and fullness are more universal than their specific forms. The opposite is also true. One type of fullness can create many forms of emptiness (3.2.5 Dynamics of Reversal).

Illustration:

Let us apply these ideas to building a small business.

1. *We must avoid the full and seek the empty.* If we run a small business, our opportunity to improve our business in a strategic sense (as opposed to operationally) exists in finding the empty places in our customers that we can fill.

2. *Emptiness and fullness can take may different forms*. Customers may want more service or less interruption. They may want lower prices or more value. They may want more selection or an easier decision.

3. *Opportunity arises from the eternal shift among different forms of emptiness and fullness.* People want what they don't have and cannot currently get. Those who have lower prices may want more value or they may want more selection. Those who have more value may want lower prices or an easier decision. They may want one or more of these forms of emptiness, depending on what they can already get.

4. The shift among emptiness and fullness cannot be exactly predicted. If a customer need is predicted, it would have likely been filled. As a business, our opportunities exist in customer needs that both we and our competitors have overlooked.

5. Emptiness becomes our opportunity when we can fill it for others. If we cannot offer more service, or sell for less or offer more selection, those forms of emptiness do not offer an opportunity for us. We must concentrate on making their decisions easier, offering more value, and offering less interruption,

6. Emptiness is a temporary state so opportunity requires speed. Rather than planning complex changes that require time to develop, we must offer quick, little changes in policy to see what strikes the right chord with customers.

7. Small empty spaces are much more common than large. Rather than trying to solve big but rare problems, we must offer little changes that address smaller but more common problems.

8. Small openings lead to larger ones. If customers see continual improvement in our operations, they will return more frequently to see what else has changed.

9. One form of emptiness can require other different forms of fullness. As we get more attention from customers, we will be able to address more and more of their needs over time.

3.2.5 Dynamic Reversal

Description: Sun Tzu's six key methods regarding how situations reverse themselves naturally.

"War is very sloppy and messy.
Positions turn around."
　　Sun Tzu's The Art of War 6:8:5 (Chinese Revealed).

"The reverse side also has a reverse side."
　　　　　　　　　　　　　　　　　Japanese Proverb

General Principle: We see opportunities by thinking backwards and upside-down.

Situation:

We are taught linear thinking but Sun Tzu's strategy is its opposite: seeing everything as a loop. We are taught that more is better, but in competition less is more. When we look at opportunities as openings, we are not looking for something but for nothing. Because of this, identifying competitive opportunities is counter intuitive. From this perspective, an opportunity never looks like an opportunity. It looks like a problem.

Opportunity:

Once we understand the nature of opportunities, we can use a simple mental trick to find them more easily. Opportunities are openings, empty spaces of unfilled potential. Since they are a form of negative space, the identification of opportunities often requires us to reverse the normal, obvious, and "common sense" everyday way that we normally see situations. This "backwards thinking" usually seems foolish until an opportunity is proven. However, once an opportunity is proven, everyone sees it as obvious.

Key Methods:

These following six key methods help us harness the dynamics of reversal.

1. We find opportunities by imagining the world reversing itself. Seeing opportunity is an act of imagination. Complementary opposites re-balance situations. Opportunities shift among different forms of emptiness and fullness. What is full today will be empty tomorrow. What is empty today will be full tomorrow (3.2.4 Emptiness and Fullness).

2. We must see every problem as an opportunity and seeming opportunities as a potential problem. If something is a problem for us, it is also probably a problem for others. All problems represent needs that must be addressed and we can get rewarded for addressing (3.2 Opportunity Creation).

3. We must envision what is old as new and what is new as if it was old. Opportunity is created by change, but change is a cycle, recycling what has come before. When people see things as new, they are missing the connection to the past. When they see it as old, they miss the connection to the future. Our opportunity is seeing what most people miss (3.2.2 Opportunity Invisibility).

4. ***We must see every strength as a weakness and every weakness as a strength***. Every coin has two sides, a positive and a negative. Since one side usually commands the attention of most people, it gets plenty of attention and cannot be an opportunity. To find the opening we need, we have to look at the other side that every one is overlooking (3.2.3 Complementary Opposites).

5. ***We must imagine doing the exactly opposite of what others do and acting where others avoid acting.*** This lesson is a little tricky because we don't want to go the wrong way on one-way streets or drive through stop lights when everyone else stops. The controlling rule here is that we must avoid costly conflict. Doing the opposite or acting when others don't is an opportunity when it eliminates conflict. It is not an opportunity when it creates conflict (3.1.3 Conflict Cost).

6. ***We must think about offering less instead of more and working slower rather than faster***. This is the ultimate in reverse thinking because it contradicts two key principles of opportunity and strategy themselves. Opportunity is filling openings. How can offering less fill a hole better than more? Speed is the essence of competition. How can going slower ever offer an advantage? However, everyone sees the value of more and more speed, even when they don't understand opportunity or strategy. This rule plays to a higher standard, that of strategic profitability. Less and slower consumes less resources creating a new potential for profitability that others often miss (3.1.2 Strategic Profitability).

Illustration:

Let us illustrate these idea in terms of investing.

1. We find opportunities by imagining the world reversing itself. While stocks may or may not be a good or bad buy right now, these principles provide a more strategic way of thinking about stock investing.

2. We must see every problem as an opportunity and seeming opportunities as a potential problem. One of the most common mistakes in investing is selling the winners and holding the losers. This is logical in the sense that selling winners makes a profit while we can wait for losers to turn around. However, it is poor investment strategy. Much better to sell losers asap and hold winners (setting stop points in case they turn around and become losers).

3. We must envision what is old as new and what is new as if it was old. When an adviser tout the latest hot stock, avoid buying it. Look for old, tire stocks (of good, solid companies, of course) that no one cares about any more. This is the logic behind the Dogs of the Dow philosophy, which have historically outperformed the Dow.

4. We must see every strength as a weakness and every weakness as a strength. A strong stock has a high price. A weak stock has a low price. If the goal is to buy low and sell high to create a profit, what do you prefer?

5. We must imagine doing the exactly opposite of what others do and acting where others avoid acting. Sell what most people are buying. Buy what most people are selling. Trade more when others are trading less. Trade less when they are trading more.

*6. We must think about offering less instead of more and working slower rather than faster.*Buy fewer stocks (or ETFs) and hold them longer. Make fewer trades after more deliberation. It is like playing poker, if you bet on every hand, you are going to lose.

3.2.6 Opening Matrix Tool

Description: Six key methods using for building a matrix to help us identify unseen openings using Sun Tzu's elements of a position.

	Climate	Mission	Ground	Leadersh	Methods
Opening Type		Unmet	Unclaimed	Missing	Needed
CHANGES	Change Reversal	Needs/ Values	Resources/ Rewards	Leader/ Decision	Methods Shift
Change 1					
Change 2					
Change 3					
Change 4					
Change 5					

"Many advantages add up to victory.
Few advantages add up to defeat."
Sun Tzu's The Art of War 1:5:5-6.

"Opportunities? They are all around us: there is power lying latent everywhere waiting for the observant eye to discover it."
Orison Swett Marden

General Principle: Analyzing the effects of various changes on the five elements of positioning reveals hidden openings.

Situation:

People have a difficult time seeing opportunities because they are looking in the wrong place. They see what is already there rather than what is missing. Nature abhors a vacuum but vacuums are invisible. They see what is being used rather than what is being overlooked for use. They are frightened by change, turning away from their uncertain future rather than turning toward it and peering into its darkness. When they do look in that darkness, they imagine monsters and phantoms rather than its potential for magic.

Opportunity:

People must adapt to change. By organizing our thoughts on change, we can see the potential for new positions that it is creating. Without change, people will continue to do what they have in the past. Change motivates them to support new positions, positions we can create from the openings created by the change. Sun Tzu's five element model offers us a new way of seeing change and its potential for the future. We can use this model as a tool for seeing what is normally hidden. Like a telescope that allows us to see what is very large but too far away to be seen with our naked eyes, this model brings reveals new universes of possibility. Like the microscope, which shows what is very close but too small to be seen, this tool allows us to see the easy path forward that is normally hidden from us.

Key Methods:

The following key methods construct a matrix that we can use to see the resources and opportunities made possible by change. The idea is to identify all possible openings in a given situation.

1. List the most important changes affect your situation in the first column of the matrix. Change is the source of all opportunities. Look for changes that have a broad impact but which are easy to overlook. These changes are the source of all future opportunities (3.2 Opportunity Creation).

2. In the column next to each change, post the ways in which its trend might reverse itself or what people expect from the change might produce the opposite effect. This column represents the effect of the Climate column. While change itself is driven by climate, a future change in the current change is also caused by the continual shifts in climate. It most people are adjusting to the current change, we can get ahead of them by preparing for that changes reversal. Sun Tzu teaches that most trends tend to reverse themselves because of balances in nature driving change (3.2.5 Dynamic Reversal).

   3. In the next column, list the new or unmet needs or values created by the change or its reversal. This is the Mission column. Meeting these needs or addressing those values is an opportunity. Others are likely to see these new needs or values are a problem rather than an opportunity. These needs and values follow an hierarchy of mission values (1.6.2 Types of Motivations).

   4. In the next column, list the unclaimed resources or rewards made possible by the change or its reversal. This is the Ground column since Ground is the source of all resources and rewards. Sometimes, we can easily fill this column with ideas for getting rewarded for addressing the needs in the previous column. However, sometimes all we can see from change is the damage it does. However, "damage" to some area also often means that resources are being made available that were, in the past, being used elsewhere. These resources are available for our use if we can imagine how to use them (7.6.1 Resource Discovery).

   5. In the next column, list the missing leadership or decisions for which the change or its reversal creates a need. This is the Leader or Commander element in Sun Tzu's model. When a number of different groups are effected by a change, all with different needs, they often are simply looking for a leader who can get them all pointed in the same direction, working together using that change. By providing that leadership, providing a vision or a project with a shared goal we can mobilize a force for positive change, we can leverage people's hunger for leadership (1.5.1 Command Leadership).

   6. In the final column, list the outdated methods or the new methods that are necessitated by the change or its reversal creates a need. This is the Methods part of Sun Tzu's model. Ideas for projects or campaign utilizing change are often more easily imagined by looking at how change outdates old methods or requires new ones (1.5.2. Group Methods).

Illustration:

This tool emulates a mental process that I personally use all the time. Recently, I have been working on community development using these ideas.

1. List the most important changes affect your situation in the first column of the matrix. Our local community 0of Shoreline (north of Seattle), has been affected by the following changes:

- Disappearance of Community Media
- Improvements in Shoreline's Main Artery
- Continued Economic Slump
- New Local Government Roles for Business Development and Events
- Local Community College in Trouble
- Donations to Non-Profits Down
- Decline in Local Service Organizations (Rotary, Kiwanis)
- Less Easy to Travel to Seattle For Events

2. In the column next to each change, post the ways in which its trend might reverse itself or what people expect from the change might produce the opposite effect. The following are potential reversals of these changes:

- New community media centered around internet
- None
- Local economy turns around
- Local Government cuts back on Business Development and Event Promotion
- College is closed down
- Donations begin to climb again
- People will begin joining local service organizations

- Government will fix travel problems to downtown Seattle

3. *In the next column, list the new or unmet needs or values created by the change or its reversal.*

- Local people need to know about community events/ Local business need advertising outlets The new look makes it possible to create a new image of city
- Local businesses need help to reach customers in and outside of city
- Local government needs ideas for "place-making" to distinguish community
- Local college needs to make money selling their unused facilities
- Worthy causes in the community are increasing need
- Local service organizations need more visibility and membership
- People in area need entertainment and events that don't require travel to Seattle downtown

4. *In the next column, list the unclaimed resources or rewards made possible by the change or its reversal.*

- Business will pay for advertising on some sort of local media
- The new highway is an advertising venue for local businesses and events
- Local business are willing to donate to causes to get visibility
- Local government has resources to help put local businesses and promote local events Local college is willing to offer their facilities to local business and service organization to generate revenue
- Local needs can be used to mobilize local interest through venues like schools
- Local service organizations are willing to offer manpower and work together on projects
- There is a market for local events and entertainment

5. *In the next column, list the missing leadership or decisions for which the change or its reversal creates a need.*

- Business need someone to give them ideas for promoting their businesses
- Those controlling signing on highway need to be convinced of community need to change policies
- Local business need to be asked to contribute
- Local government needs to be given some ideas in terms of how to promote the city
- The college president and administration needs to be given some ideas about how to utilize their facilities
- The local charities need to be contacted and contribute assets such as mailing lists.
- Local service organizations need to be contacted and lead to join together.
- The local market needs to offered a series of entertaining events put on by non-profits and local businesses to support local charities and bring business into the area.

6. In the final column, list the outdated methods or the new methods that are necessitated by the change or its reversal creates a need.

- All groups (local businesses, service organizations, local government, charity organizations, local college) need to develop methods for putting on a series of local events that they can grow year after years, following the example of other communities that have built successful events attracting dollars and attention from the surrounding area.

3.3.0 Opportunity Resources

Description: Sun Tzu's eight key methods regarding the nature of the excess resources needed to fill openings.

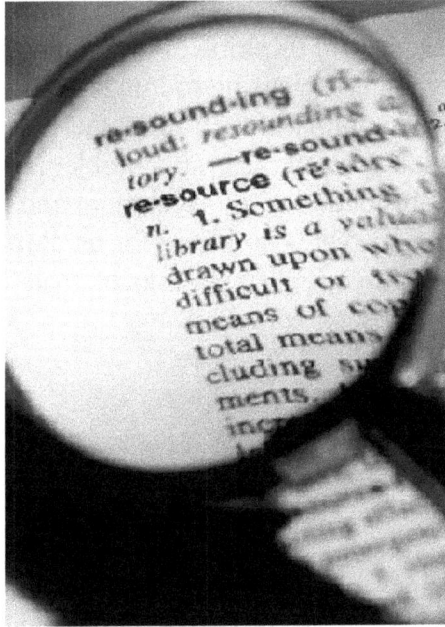

"If you are too weak to fight, you must find more men. In this situation, you must not act aggressively."
Sun Tzu's The Art of War 9:6:1-2

"The courage to imagine the otherwise is our greatest resource, adding color and suspense to all our life."
Daniel J. Boorstin

General Principle: We must pursue opportunities only when excess resources are available.

Situation:

There is a downside in learning to see openings. We can get sucked into situations that we should avoid. An opening has power. As Aristotle first observed , a vacuum pulls us in. How susceptible we are to this problem depends upon our character, but we all have a number of natural tendencies that create the problem. The first is known simply as wishful thinking , our tendency to make decisions based upon what it is pleasing to imagine. We also tend to over estimate our own ability to restrain ourselves. In research, this problem is known as restraint bias. This problem is amplified irrational escalation , our tendency to invest more and more in a past decision, even when it creates problems for us. Pursuing opportunities without understanding the constraints of basic positioning can be extremely dangerous.

Opportunity:

All openings are opportunities for someone, but we are interesting only in openings that represent our opportunities. Seeing openings in emptiness and need is a powerful and valuable skill (3.2.4 Emptiness and Fullness). We work at it because openings are so difficult to see (3.2.2 Opportunity Invisibility). Our success, however, depends upon keeping our priorities straight and seeing the big picture of our situation (2.5 The Big Picture). Knowing a few simple principles in looking for opportunities helps us protect our limited resources and helps us recognize which of these opportunities are right for us (2.1.1 Information Limits).

Key Methods:

An opening is a necessary condition for us to pursue an opportunity, but it is not a sufficient one. In addition to an opening, we obviously need the complementary resources necessary to fill that opening. The following mental model must guide us in knowing when to act and when not to.

1. We need enough resources to pursue an opportunity. Everything requires resources. It requires resources for us to maintain our existing position. It also takes resources to explore any opportunity. It may not take a lot of resources, but some resources are always required. The problems is that our resources are always limited (3.1.1 Resource Limitations).

2. We must <u>not</u> act if we do not have "excess" resources. Defense of our existing position always has the first claim on our available resources. Excess resources are those that we don't need to sustain the key aspect of our current position. When we don't have the excess resources, we must concentrate simply on defending our current position. (1.1.2 Defending Positions).

3. We must often readjust our priorities to create excess resources. Our resources are devoted to all sorts of things, all of which we can describe as "maintaining our position." When an opportunity comes along--and often before--we often must sacrifice one desire in order to get the resources to pursue a more important desire. This is always a matter of priorities, but we will never pursue any opportunity if we don't have a high priority on improving our position rather than simply maintaining it (1.6.3 Shifting Priorities).

4. We can improve our internal production to create excess resources. We perform our existing responsibilities more efficiently to generate the excess resources we need. This falls within our span of control. The more productive we are, the more resources we free up for using in competition, which is outside of our control (1.9 Competition and Production).

5. Our excess resources must fit <u>all</u> the requirements of the opportunity. Openings are the hole. Our resources are the peg. The peg must fit the hole. Opportunities often require several different types of resources, both temporary resources and physical resources. If our excess resources only match some of what is required, we must avoid the opportunity because it will inevitably take vital resources needed to maintain our current position (3.2.3 Complementary Opposites).

6. We must have excess resources at the right time. Opportunities are limited. We cannot control when openings appear or how long they last. Having or making the resources required depends largely on the timing involved. Unlike temporary resources, we can save up physical resources so they are available when opportunities appear (3.1.6 Time Limitations).

7. We must resist event pressure in evaluating our resources. Events, especially events that create opportunities, pressure us to act, even when it isn't in our best interest. We cannot act simply because of event pressure. We must act because our situation requires action (5.1.1 Event Pressure

8. When we have excess resources, we _must_ act on a high probability opportunity. We cannot act without an opportunity. We cannot act without excess resources. We must act when we have both the opportunity and the resources when there is a high-probability of our action being successful (4.0 Leveraging Probability).

Illustration:

Let us illustrate these principles in thinking about how we can expand our current responsibilities to get a promotion or work toward getting a promotion.

1. We need enough resources to pursue an opportunity. Expanding our current responsibilities requires time and effort. It is emotionally demanding. We must have the time and energy to do more without decreasing our overall performance.

2. We must _not_ act if we do not have "excess" resources. In our career, our first priority is performing our current responsibilities well. We cannot get promoted if we hurt our current performance in pursuing a promotion. If we decrease our existing job performance, we create an opening for others to attack us. If we cannot do our existing job well, we will not be given more responsibilities.

3. We must often readjust our priorities to create excess resources. We can easily be spending time on tasks that are really a part of our responsibility and aren't helping us get promoted because the need for them is not recognized by others.

4. *We can improve our internal production to create excess resources.* We need to find faster, easier ways of performing our current responsibilities. Aside from freeing up our resources, finding faster ways to work qualifies us for promotion.

5. *Our excess resources must fit all the requirements of the opportunity.* We shouldn't pursue opportunities at work for which we really aren't qualified either objectively or subjectively. In my career, I was promoted an average of every eight months and when I reach a level where I had to "pay my dues" by just doing time in my current position before being qualified for promotion, I would move to another company.

6. *We must have excess resources at the right time.* We cannot control when jobs open up. We have to be ready and positioned to take over those responsibilities when they do.

7. *We must resist event pressure in evaluating our resources.* We shouldn't just go after another position because it opens up. It must fit our skills and goals.

8. *When we have excess resources, we must act on a high probability opportunity.* If we can satisfy our existing job responsibilities with plenty of time and energy left over, we ***must*** use our excess time to pursue additional responsibilities of some kind. There are always valuable things that need doing. We must identify those that are most likely to advance us and go after them. If we don't pursue additional responsibilities, others will eventually notice that we are underemployed. This again, hurts our existing position.

3.4.0 Dis-Economies of Scale

Description: Sun Tzu's six key methods on opportunities created by the size of others.

"Small forces are not powerful.
However, large forces cannot catch them."
Sun Tzu's The Art of War 3:3:19-20

"Strength does not come from physical capacity. It comes from an indomitable will."
Mahatma Gandhi

General Principle: The size of large organizations must create opportunities for smaller organizations.

Situation:

One of the most common reasons that we fail to recognize opportunities is that we tend to think of size as an advantage. When we see a large organization, we think that it naturally dominates its competitive area. We talk about the power of economies of scale. Our expectations regarding the value of size are constantly frustrated as one large company after another fails, while new smaller companies rise up to take their place. What is happening? Our problem is that we fail to understand most of the advantages of size are advantages in production, not competition. While size is a great advantage in any controlled areas of production, as an areas of contention becomes more and more competitive, size turns into a disadvantage.

Opportunity:

Competitive opportunities are openings. The actions of large competitors tend to create new openings, but most of these openings are too small for the large competitor themselves. As we master Sun Tzu's principles, we see that every characteristic, especially size, has both advantages and disadvantages (3.2.4 Emptiness and Fullness). In competitive arenas, size advantages turn into weaknesses that we can exploit. Dominant large organizations change the environment but, in doing so, they become easy targets for smaller, more adaptable competitors. One of the secrets in identifying opportunities is studying the nature of the large organizations. The advance of their position drives out smaller direct competitors in markets they move into, but that advance also creates a whole new set of openings in their wake.

Key Methods:

The following key methods describe how the large size of a competitor creates opportunities for smaller competitors.

1. The same size that is an advantage in production is a disadvantage in competitive maneuvering. The skills of production and competitive adaptability are complementary opposites. Size creates advantages in production. For this reason, small organizations cannot meet large ones in contests determined by productive capacity. This advantage in production, however, necessarily creates competitive disadvantages in adapting to change. Large ones cannot keep up with small ones in adapting to change (3.2.3 Complementary Opposites).

2. *Momentum creates two types of large organizations and two types of opportunities*. An organization doesn't get large without developing a great deal of momentum. Vital organizations with great momentum create opportunities by reshaping the competitive landscape, opening up new ground for new smaller organizations. However, all momentum fades over time. Large organizations with fading momentum encourages a new crop of competitors in the areas that they once controlled. These competitors feed off the fading organization (7.5 Momentum Limitations).

3. *Large organizations create sameness which creates the need for variety*. During their vital growth stage, the productive power of large organizations drive out the smaller, more varied, but less productive organizations. In doing so, they create a more homogeneous environment. This new environment is never perfect. It comes with a new set of unmet needs. These needs are small at first, easier for small organization's to see and address (3.2 Opportunity Creation)

4. *Strength comes from unity and focus rather than size*. People mistakenly think that size is strength. The larger an organization is, the more problems it has with unity and focus. Different parts of the organization develop separate missions and what benefits one part of the organization can be very destructive to other parts. This is especially true in the internal competition for resources between new growing parts that represent the future and the older established parts the create the most resources (1.7 Internal Strength).

5. *Loss of unity and focus creates openings*. If we think in terms of strategic positions, the problems with size become apparent. Larger organizations cover more ground, but they cannot be equally strong everywhere. Their size also slows them down, making it very difficult for them to change direction and stay united (3.4.1 Unity Breakdown).

6. Size limits opportunity. Size also makes it more difficult to find suitable new positions. Small opportunities are more common than large opportunities. The larger an organization's size, the rarer suitable opportunities are. Most openings are too small to provide them with meaningful opportunities. As their existing positions naturally degrade overtime, large organizations find it difficult to find new positions to accommodate them. This forces them into less and less profitable and tenable competitive arena (3.4.2 Opportunity Fit).

7. Size makes large organizations slow to react to change. Their size also slows them down, making it more and more diffi-cult for them to change direction. Changing direction and keeping united is even more difficult. The decision loop through the organi-zation's hierarchy takes more time in large organizations than small ones. As changes come both from the environment and from com-petitive challenges, large organizations are slow to react. This slow reaction also creates opportunities for competitors (3.4.3 Reaction Lag).

Illustration:

I am tempted to give examples from military history such as Alex-ander the Great, leading a force of less than 40,000 destroying Darius's Persian army estimated to be about 600,000 in the Battle at Issus , but let us look at some modern business examples that are easier to appre-ciate.

1. The same size that is an advantage in production is a disad-vantage in competitive maneuvering. When IBM was big, Micro-soft could outmaneuver them. When Microsoft was big, Google could outmaneuver them.

2. Momentum creates two types of large organizations and two types of opportunities. Google and Apple create new markets in the building momentum phase. Others such as Microsoft and WalMart are still growing, but coasting on their momentum. The vast majority are companies such as Sears, GE, AIG, Citibank, NY Times, etc. whose momentum has faded and are passing away.

3. Large organizations create sameness which creates the need for variety. The standard environment created by Microsoft Windows created a huge application market for PCs. We are about to see the same thing take place again for Google's Android phones.

4. Strength comes from unity and focus rather than size. 70-80% of new jobs are created by small businesses, not large. Over any twenty years, about 80% of the Fortune 500 of America's largest companies is replaced.

5. Loss of unity and focus creates openings. Starbuck's just brought out an instant coffee, which it is selling hard. This is creating a rift within the company and between the company and its customers. ***Size creates limitations.*** When Starbuck's started opening stores across the street from each other, we should have seen the writing on the wall.

6. Size makes large organizations slow to react to change. Merck's slow reaction to news of heart problems from their arthritis drug Vioxx in 2004 created legal problems that continue today.

3.4.1 Unity Breakdown

Description: Sun Tzu's eight key methods regarding the conflict between size and unity.

"Another [commander] has subcommanders who are angry and defiant; they attack the enemy and fight their own battles."
Sun Tzu's The Art of War 10:2:17

"United we stand, divided we fall."
George Pope Morris

General Principle: Growth in the size of an organization naturally decreases its unity and focus.

Situation:

The mistake is thinking that size equals strength. We think of size in competition like children on a playground. Those who are bigger can bully. We want to get big so we won't be bullied. Because we are taught linear thinking , this seems to make sense. The problem is that competition doesn't follow the same rules of scale. Strength in competition is not defined by size. We think that if we grow, competition will get easier but it often gets more difficult. Size works against the real source of strength in competition. Large competitors can be intimidating, but they cannot be strong in the way that Sun Tzu defines strength.

Opportunity:

When we understand the problems of size, we learn to leverage the size of our opponents against them. Sun Tzu teaches that strength comes from a strongly shared mission not from size. From a single, clear mission flows focus and unity, which are the true components of strength. While the key elements that make up a strategic position are the same for any size organization (13.2 Element Scalability), strength from focus and unity does not scale. Opportunities are openings, arising from need, but all openings and needs are limited in size (3.2 Opportunity Creation). Eating one ice-cream sundae is good. Eating two isn't necessarily better. Eating ten is a form of torture.

Key Methods:

The following seven key methods describe how we look for opportunities in unity breakdown.

1. The first place we look for opportunities is in where unity and focus breaks down. Unity and focus are the source of strength. Strength arises from our shared mission, but because mission is the core of all strategic positions, a breakdown of unity and focus affects all five key aspects of a position. The larger the organization, the harder it is to maintain focus and unity. This creates weakness, which is an opportunity for others (1.7 Competitive Strength).

2. As organizations grow, smaller groups within them separate themselves. Each separate need that an organization fills has a limited size. Large organizations grow by serving many needs. Growth creates multiple missions. Different missions divide large organizations. We use the word "divisions" to describe the internal separations in of large organizations. These divisions naturally separate to create weakness within the organization (1.6.1 Shared Mission).

3. The logical division of labor requires internal connections that can break down. The division of labor depends on both loose and tight internal couplings. Over time, this integration tends to break down. Individuals focus their groups immediate goals, drifting away from the shared mission for practical reasons. This is known in management science as "practical drift" in business methods (1.5.2. Group Methods).

4. Division weakens the power of a mission. The larger the organization, the more basic its mission becomes. Different divisions find the lowest common denominator of mission. This is also the weakest of missions. In a business, it ends up as "making money." This makes the large organization generic, blurring its distinction from the rest of its competitive arena. Without a clear mission, it is held together only by history and structure, losing the impact of focus (1.7.2 Goal Focus).

5. Division leads to weak, spread-out positions. As missions diverge, different missions lead part of the organizations in different directions. The organization's focus gets spread out over more and more ground. The different systems in the organization no longer support each other. As Sun Tzu said, an army that tries to defend everywhere is weak everywhere. An organization that does more and more things does them less and less well (4.6.1 Extremes of Area).

6. Different internal goals lead inevitably to internal battles for resources. Size is an advantage in production. This means that large organizations have more resources, but divided missions mean different priorities. Different priorities create battles within an organization over limited resources (1.6.3 Shifting Priorities).

7. Internal competition takes the place of external competition. This takes the form of internal politics. Politics emerges with growth as different groups develop their own separate agendas. More and more people within the organization can gain more personally from winning internal battles than external ones. Since these battles are internal, conflict becomes unavoidable. Since conflict is the most costly aspect of competition, the costs of running the organization rises inexplicably as more resources and energy are lost in internal conflict (3.1.3 Conflict Cost)

8. Opportunity for smaller competitors exists in all these divisions. Opportunity exists in openings. Large competitors create the need for more focused competitors, with clearer, sharper missions. Those competitors can take advantage of the openings on the ground created by weak, spread out positions. They can better use their resources by avoiding battle and focusing on external progress (3.1.4 Openings).

Illustration:

This problem with unity and focus and growth is seen most clearly in the growth of government.

1. The first place we look for opportunities is in where unity and focus breaks down. Both parties are in the process of discovering that larger government is less effective government. The Republicans lost their unity and focus during the Bush years. The Democrats are losing their unity and focus during Obama's presidency despite overwhelming majorities in both houses of Congress.

2. As organizations grow, smaller groups within them separate themselves. The Republicans are trying to decide if they are the small government party or simply large government "light". The Democrats, meanwhile, are fighting over whether or not universal health care must be provided for abortions and illegal aliens.

3. The logical division of labor requires internal connections that can break down. Rules allowing members of both parties to work together have been established over the years to prevent the dominant party from over-stepping their mandate. These rules protected minority interests from being shut out of debate and the majority from power plays that alienate the public. For example, the requirement in the Senate for 60 votes for cloture. However, over the years both parties have lost sight of the value of those rules.

4. Growth weakens the power of mission. The growth of government has blurred America's founding principles based on protecting individual liberty at home and fighting for it abroad. The big political tent is, by definition, a hard mission to package. Generic missions such as "change" quickly devolve into specific questions such as "change into what?"

5. Division leads to weak, spread-out positions. These weakness demonstrates itself on how poorly the government executes every activity. Politicians complain when corporation make a measly few percentage points in profit creating goods and services, but the government cannot give away $8,000 for used cars without it costing taxpayers over $30,000 per vehicle.

6. Different internal goals creates internal battles for resources. Politicians of both parties seem less and less interested in passing good laws and more and more interested in buying political support at the taxpayers expense. No one needs to read the legislation anymore as long as they know it has their own personal earmarks in it. For each billion dollars a politician gives out in taxpayer money, they want to see a million come back to them in political donations or cheap loans or free vacation homes.

7. Internal competition takes the place of external competition. As government tries to "solve more problems" within the country, America grows weaker in its world position both economically and militarily. In the recent decision to hold 9/11 trials in NY , America's enemies are given the publicity that they want so that one political party can put the other political party on trial.

8. Opportunity for smaller competitors exists in all these divisions. As America is more consumed with its own political divisions, it becomes more and more a target for terrorist and economic attack.

3.4.2 Opportunity Fitness

Description: Sun Tzu's seven key methods describing the problems for large organization finding new opportunities that fit their size.

"Victory comes from correctly using both large and small forces."

Sun Tzu's The Art of War 3:5:3

"Small opportunities are often the beginning of great enterprises."

Demosthenes

General Principle: Larger organizations have more difficulty finding high-probability opportunities suitable for their size.

Situation:

Just as we confuse size with strength, we also confuse size with our capabilities to pursue opportunities. Because we are taught to think that bigger is better, we think of larger organizations as having more opportunities. The competitive reality is much more complicated. We can get into serious trouble if we fail to understand how our size relative to our competition sets practical limits on the opportunities that we can pursue.

Opportunity:

When we understand how our relative size affects our opportunities, we can identify suitable opportunities more easily. Opportunities are openings that fit our available strategic resources (3.1.1 Resource Limitations). Our resources have both size and shape. As with all competitive characteristics, the size and shape of our resources is relative. We only understand our qualities by comparing them against the position of our potential competitors (1.3.1 Competitive Comparison). Our relative size compared to our potential competitors creates both problems and opportunities in terms of finding opportunities that fit our resources.

Key Methods:

The following seven key methods describe the problems in finding opportunities that fit larger organizations.

1. ***Opportunity fit comes from matching available resources to the size and shape of openings.*** Large organizations are more likely to have a large variety of available resources but fewer opportunities to use them. Small organization are less likely to have a variety of available resources but many more opportunities to use them (3.3 Opportunity Resources).

2. ***Openings can be too large or too small to fit an opportunity.*** Successfully pursuing openings that are too big for our resources simply paves the way for larger competitors. Pioneering openings

that have too little long-term potential relative to the overall size of the organization leads to fragmentation. A number of small opportunities does not equal a big opportunity because the organization that pursues them pulls itself apart (3.4.1 Unity Breakdown).

3. Small opportunities fit our resources best when we are close to them. The vast majority of opportunities are small, local ones. These opportunities are the open spaces left between and among other existing positions. These opportunities fit our resources best when we are close to them physically or psychologically. Fit is based on proximity and affinity. Existing positions that are too distant from the need either physically or psychologically do not fit (4.4 Strategic Distance).

4. Large openings only arise on frontiers and fit those closest to them. A frontier is a new competitive arena opened by new methods. There are two common general types of frontiers. ***Frontiers for exploration*** arise when new methods open up entirely new areas of unknown potential. ***Frontiers for consolidation*** arise when new methods create the means for a large organization to displace a number of smaller, more diversified, local organizations. Both require the use of innovation. (7.3 Strategic Innovation).

5. The potential on frontiers of exploration is unknown but it always starts small. When a new competitive area is opened up by new methods, knowledge, or technology, its true potential is unknown, but it always starts out small. While some large organization's can pioneer new areas, the size of most of these opportunities will never be large and those that are large enough will take a long time to develop. Because of internal competition for resources, most mature large organization's do not have the patience to develop them (3.1.6 Time Limitations).

6. The potential on the frontiers of consolidation are better known but also usually start small. Since consolidation transforms an existing competitive arena, the general size of that arena is known. Successful consolidation almost always requires specialized knowledge only available within a competitive area. Consolidation is started by a small organization within that arena pioneering new methods that make consolidation possible. Large competitors can seldom move into an arena ripe for consolidation from the outside because they lack the specific knowledge and skills required (2.6 Knowledge Leverage).

*7. **People within large organizations are less capable at perceiving risks.*** Responsibility becomes more diffused in groups. People in groups make riskier decisions than they would ever make alone because they perceive that the others in the group are approving of that risk taking. This is known in psychology as the "risky shift." Coupled with fewer natural opportunities, this risky shift leads large organizations to pursue low probability opportunities instead of high-probability ones (4.0 Leveraging Probability).

Illustration:

Let us look at some business examples from the modern world.

*1. **Opportunity fit comes from matching available resources to the size and shape of openings.*** One example is Warren Buffett's investment firm, Berkshire Hathaway. Historically, Berkshire Hathaway grew by acquiring privately held firms. However, as Berkshire Hathaway has grown in scale, there are simply fewer and fewer companies larger enough for it to pursue. Buffett has discussed this problem a number of times, as this recent article describes: Buffett deals only with large companies because he needs to make massive investments to garner the returns required to post excellent results for the huge size to which his company, Berkshire Hathaway, has grown.

*2. **Openings can be too large or too small to fit an opportunity.*** See specific examples below.

*3. **Small opportunities fit our resources best when we are close to them.*** Here is a typical example in the pharmaceutical industry, described in an article in the The Atlantic about how the mergers in the industry is eliminating the availability of new drugs: At large companies, products that are technically promising are terminated if the marketing potential is thought to be too small. And the height of that market hurdle has risen as the profits of the large companies have grown. Today, programs that are thought to have an annual sales potential of less than $1 billion are usually stopped in their tracks. Some companies have abandoned their work in entire areas of medicine, such as antibiotics, because they believe the markets are too small to make a difference to their total sales.

4. Large openings only arise on frontiers and fit those closest to them. Frontiers for exploration are new markets such as the personal computer or internet market. Frontiers for consolidation occur in places like retailing where new innovation in communication and transportation created new methods of distribution.

5. The potential on frontiers of exploration is unknown but it always starts small. A number of large companies were directly involved in the pioneering efforts to create the first personal computers. IBM, Digital Equipment, and Xerox all did the basic research in development but lost out to relative new comers like Apple because they were all too big for the opportunity. IBM's first successful PC (after a series of failures) was more of a success for the small companies Microsoft and Intel than it was for IBM who, of course, eventually sold off its PC division. The same was true in the Internet, where large media companies such as Time/Warner invested heavily buying AOL. The result again was spectacular failure.

6. The potential on the frontiers of consolidation are better known but also usually start small. It was Wal-Mart and Costco, coming from nowhere, who revolutionized retail distribution, not the giants Sears JC Penney's, or K-Mart. Enron was very successful at consolidating the trading of energy in the form of natural gas contracts, but when they moved outside their area of expertise into other forms of trading, such as broadband contracts, the result was a spectacular financial failure and collapse.

7. People within large organizations are less capable at perceiving risks. How could Enron get into so much trouble? Inherently risky decisions were perceived as less risky because of the size of the group that seemingly approved of them.

3.4.3 Reaction Lag

Description: Sun Tzu's six key methods regarding why organizations react slower as they grow larger.

""*Take advantage of a larger enemy's inability to keep up.*

Sun Tzu's The Art of War 11:2.17

"The percentage of mistakes in quick decisions is no greater than in long-drawn-out vacillation, and the effect of decisiveness itself 'makes things go' and creates confidence."

Anne O'Hare McCormick

General Principle: The larger the organization, the slower its reaction time.

Situation:

Speed is the essence of competition. In any organization, the reactive decisions are made on the frontlines, reacting to external events. What happens to reaction time as an organization grows? Its ability to react to external events slows down. The problem in larger organizations is the coordination of response. The larger the organization, the more entangled its lines of authority. More levels of decision-makers are involved. Different parts of the organization will react to events in very different ways. While strategy arises from our reaction to external stimulus, for large organizations, that reaction becomes an internal problem.

Opportunity:

The opportunity here is for relatively small organizations to take advantage of events before their larger competitors can react. The opportunity for larger organizations is use their advantages in resources to overcome their disadvantages in initial response. Large organizations create opportunities for smaller organizations because they are, by necessity, slower to react to events. For both, the use of strategy depends heavily on speed and quickness.

Key Methods:

The basis of good strategy is fast cycle-times (1.8.3 Cycle Time). Events are happening continuously. Sun Tzu adapts to those events. Our initial response are never perfect, but the faster our reaction cycles, the more quickly we can fine-turn our response. Quick reactions cycles, even if imperfect, can make situations more difficult for our opponents (5.3 Reaction Time).

1. Internal areas of control always grow faster than external competitive interfaces. Growing an organization is like blowing up a balloon. The surface of the balloon is the competitive interface where the organization makes contact with the environment. The internal volume of the balloon is the organization's span of control.

As an organization grows, its competitive surface expands but its span of control expands much, much faster. This is mathematically true for any solid object. For a sphere, the surface grows at the rate of its size squared, but the volume grows at the rate of its size cubed (1.9 Competition and Production).

2. The demands of internal control move the organization's focus toward _executing plans._ Large organizations require more internal planning because they have a large interior volume of production resources. Production requires planning, but the focus on internal planning decreases the focus on external strategy. Those on the competitive surface of the organization must increasingly conform their decisions to existing plans. Sales plans and marketing plans have little predictive value aside from extending historical momentum into the future but they are necessary to feed production planning (1.9.2 Span of Control).

3. Existing plans slows down reaction time to unplanned external events. As planning comes to dominate organizational thinking, both recognizing external events and adjusting to them requires more time. Actions must be coordinated to plans. The minority of people who are concerned about strategy are outnumbered by the volume of people who are concerned about maintaining plans (5.2.1 Choosing Adaptability).

4. Front-line decision-makers may see what needs to be done but cannot make the case to do it quickly. Managers throughout the company have not been trained in strategy. Instead they are consciously trained to make decisions within a narrow set of boundaries. This means when unexpected events arise, front-line decision-makers are at a disadvantage as the decision is passed up through the organization hierarchy and out to different divisions within the organization. The more unusual the event, the further up the hierarchy it must go for a decision to be made (3.4.1 Unity Breakdown).

5. Information degrades as it moves through the organization decreasing decision pressure. This means that more than time is lost in clarifying what is really happening. The further decision-makers are from the front-lines, the more time it takes them to gather information about an event in order to develop a complete picture of the situation. The more people through whom information and decisions must pass, the more likely it is to hit a bottleneck or simply get lost or forgotten (2.1.1 Information Limits)

6. *Organizations are trained to execute plans not to adapt to changing conditions*. Larger armies must train their people how to change directions quickly, but other large organizations are not similarly trained. Once a decision is made, large organization's take longer to act than small ones. Coordinating large groups always takes longer than coordinating small groups. A small group of twenty people can put together a task force of five people many times more quickly than a larger group can. A useful rule of thumb to calculate the relative time of response is simply to multiply response time by the relative difference in size. If one group is twice as large as another, it will take them twice as long to respond. If it is a hundred times longer, it will take them a hundred times longer to respond to an unforeseen event (6.0 Situation Response).

Illustration:

The best example of this problem of reaction lag is in the growth of government and its delivery of services.

1. *Internal areas of control always grow faster than external competitive interfaces.* When a government is small and local, most its resources are on the surface. The elected officials deal directly with the public that they serve on a hourly basis, providing many services directly themselves. As the government grows, not only are the elected officials more and more isolated but more and more government employees work inside increasingly large bureaucracies with no public contact at all.

2. *The demands of internal control move the organization's focus toward executing plans.* As government grows larger, more and more people are devoted to writing policies, regulations, and

plans. The laws themselves grow in volume and size until they are so complex that no one understands them.

3. Existing plans slows down reaction time to unplanned external events. Regulations become so confused that Treasury Secretary Geithner, who is responsible for the tax code, cannot correctly pay his income tax and Attorney General Holder cannot answer the question about whether or not those who capture bin Laden would have to read him his Miranda rights.

4. Front-line decision-makers may see what needs to be done but cannot make the case to do it quickly. Top decision-makers are largely immune from the consequences of their mistakes, but those on the front-line know that they will be held responsible for their decisions. Making decisions requires more and more diffusion on responsibility to avoid the consequences of the complex internal environment.

5. Information degrades as it moves through the organization decreasing decision pressure. Incumbents and bureaucrats are increasingly isolated from the decisions that they make, so they feel that they can concentrate on issues such as medical care and cap-and-trade, while the economy and dollar spirals downward.

6. Organizations are trained to execute plans not to adapt to changing conditions. While large companies usually punished by the market for their increasingly ineffective organizations, government simply sends tax payers a bigger and bigger bill.

3.5.0 Strength and Weakness

Description: Sun Tzu's six key methods explain how openings created by the strength of others.

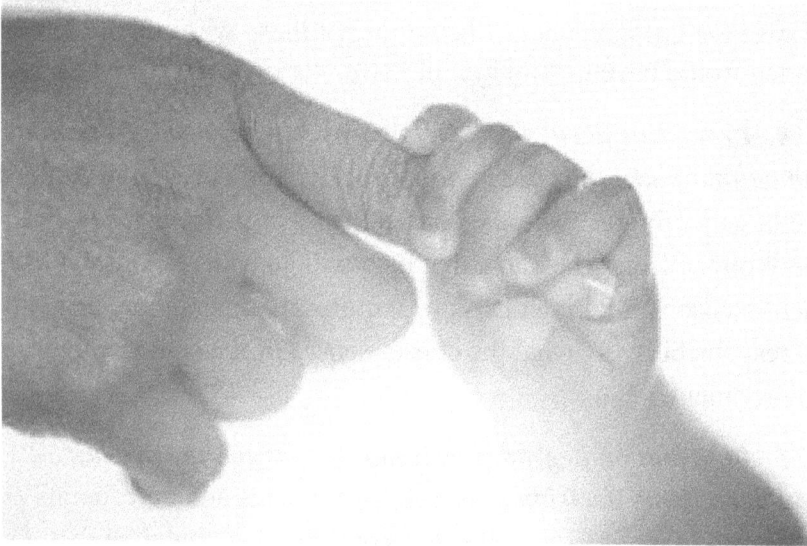

""You must adapt to opportunities and weaknesses."
Sun Tzu's The Art of War 8:2:2

"If you think a weakness can be turned into a strength, I hate to tell you this, but that's another weakness."
Jack Handy

General Principle: A competitor's strength always creates a corresponding weakness that is an opening.

Situation:

Strength draws our attention. We naturally focus on the strengths of others. One of the most common strategic mistakes is thinking that we have to duplicate the strengths of others in order to be competitive. Nothing is further from the truth. Though we are a thousand times more likely to hear about the strengths of others, especially our rivals, than we are their weaknesses, this doesn't mean that our success lies in copying them. That path only leads to duplication of effort and often to conflict as a test of similar relative strengths.

Opportunity:

Our opportunity is not in duplicating the strengths of others but in complementing them. It is the weaknesses of others that creates openings and our opportunities. Openings are difficult to see directly because people hide their weaknesses (3.2.2 Opportunity Invisibility). While people disguise their weaknesses, their strengths are easy to see and seldom disguised. Our opportunity is that we can use those strengths to identify their weaknesses. Every strength creates a corresponding weakness if we know where to look for it. It is these weaknesses that provide us with our opportunities. They are the openings that we can take leverage to our advantage. Learning how to identify weaknesses in strengths takes time and practice. Once we master these skills, every time a strength draws our attention, we can instantly find ourselves thinking about the weaknesses that this strength could engender.

Key Methods:

Weakness arises from strength in the specific ways described by the following key methods.

1. We never look for advantage by duplicating a rival's strengths. Duplicating strengths looks easier than it is. Such duplication alone cannot result in a superior position because it is a copy. At best, it creates a good copy, a second-best position. It also usually fails on economic grounds, because our rivals are always ahead of us on the learning curve (3.1.2 Strategic Profitability).

2. We can use people's strengths to predict their behavior and predictability is a weakness. People use their strengths and tend to develop their strengths over time. Once we understand where a position's strength lies, we can predict how it will be used and how it develops over time. We can also better predict what surrounding positions will be left open (2.3.2 Reaction Unpredictability).

3. *Ground area, barriers, and stickiness each create two balancing forms of weaknesses*. These three dimensions determine the "surface" characteristics of a strategic position. Each of their six extremes creates a different specific form of weakness (4.7 Competitive Weaknesses).

4. *For decision makers, character excesses generate weaknesses*. Sun Tzu describes five key characteristics of decision makers. We normally think of a weakness as a lack, but Sun Tzu teaches that excessive strength creates weaknesses. This is especially true when we look at a person's character. We can find opportunities in the specific weaknesses of character--over-confidence, foolhardiness, indecision, rigidity, and fussiness--arise from an excess of certain traits (4.7.1 Command Weaknesses).

5. *Imbalances within organizations create weaknesses*. An organization needs a balances of skills and capabilities. An overbalance in one area or another creates an organization weakness. Sun Tzu describes six specific forms of imbalances. We learn those weaknesses in order to spot the opportunities that they create (4.7.2 Group Weaknesses).

6. *Specific forms of strength generate specific forms of weakness*. We look for our openings by identifying the flip side of a given strength. Sun Tzu's principles list many specific forms of strength and their corresponding weakness. Fast service is good, but it means limited choices and quality. Having lot of options is good, but more options make decisions more difficult. Low prices are good, but it means less quality and service. High quality and service is good, but it means high prices. The most common example of this are the weaknesses caused by size (3.4 Dis-Economies of Scale).

7. *More generally, we can use the calculus of emptiness and fullness to find weakness in strength*. A strength is a fullness of some resource. Every resource is generated buy a key element of a position (1.3 Elemental Analysis). Every key element is balanced by an opposing element. A surplus in one side of the equation creates a corresponding cost on the other side of the equation (3.2.4 Emptiness and Fullness).

Illustration:

Since this is such a broad topic, let us look at a variety of examples here.

1. We never look for advantage by duplicating a rival's strengths. For example, Apple is a great proprietary design company. In trying to duplicate Apple's success, a lot of competitors will focus on trying to out-design Apple. In taking this path, virtually all of them will fail. Apple's position as the design leader is firmly established both by objective facts and subjective beliefs. No one will change it until Apple starts making consistent mistakes in design (like the recessed headphones jack of the first iPhone).

2. We can use people's strengths to predict their behavior and predictability is a weakness. As self-defense martial artist once explained to me, you always know exactly where the focus of an armed attacker is. It is focused on his weapon and his weapon hand. He is vulnerable everywhere else because his attention is consumed by the weapon. His strength is his vulnerability.

3. Ground area, barriers, and stickiness create specific forms of weaknesses. The highly successful position of Coke was based on its "secret recipe," and that positioning is extremely sticky, which is usually considered a good thing because people are devoted to sticky positions. Pepsi took advantage of that stickiness by catering to changing tastes offering a sweeter product and using taste tests to promote that product. Coke could not counter that move with its own sweeter product because of the stickiness of its position, as it discovered with its failed introduction of New Coke,

4. For decision makers, character excesses generate weaknesses. Historically, highly educated and academically intelligent state leaders have been characteristically flawed throughout modern history by indecision, especially in choosing between two bad alternatives when no good alternatives are available.

5. Imbalances within organizations create weaknesses. We commonly see larger organizations grow their internal bureaucracies until they become like GM: unable to respond to market competition because their decisions are too heavily influenced by internal issues.

6. Specific forms of strength generate specific forms of weakness. For example, after years in the software business, when I hear about how "feature rich" a software product is, I instantly think about the downsides of features. More features make it difficult to learn those features. Features often get in the way of the relatively simple tasks. Features cost money to develop and support and increase the costs of software.

7. More generally, we can use the calculus of emptiness and fullness to find weakness in strength. Going back to our example of Apple, the strength of great design creates weaknesses. Great design is costly. Products that provide the same functionality can be built and sold much less expensively. Those who compete with Apple on price will always find a place in the market because Apple will never see themselves as the low-cost producer.

3.6.0 Leveraging Subjectivity

Description: Sun Tzu's seven key methods regarding openings between subjective and objective positions.

*""You can be as mysterious as the fog.
You can strike like sounding thunder."*

Sun Tzu's The Art of War 7:3:7-8

"It isn't what we don't know that gets us in trouble. It is what we think we know that ain't so."

Will Rodgers

General Principle: Many opportunities arise in the gap between objective reality and subjective perception.

Situation:

An opportunity requires two components: an opening in the environment and the resources to move into it. These resources take many different forms. A new job requires qualifications. A new business requires investment. The problem is that all resources are limited. Our resource limitations are especially a problem when we are first starting out, but, even as we advance, it always seems that each additional step forward always requires more resources than the last. The use of physical resources is like the use of force. The more force we use, the more resistance we meet.

Opportunity:

Our opportunity is in replacing the use of physical resources with intellectual leverage. We can leverage people's perceptions of our position to advance our position. There is always a gap between the objective reality and people's subjective opinions. That gap is a special type of opening that we can use as an opportunity (3.1.4 Openings). Our position is like a bottle. Since we are inside the bottle, we cannot read its label. Others can read the label, but they don't really know what is inside the bottle. All they know is what the label says. Changing the label to improve people's perceptions is easier than changing the contents of the bottle. We use this change in packaging as a leverage point to change our objective position (2.6 Knowledge Leverage).

Key Methods:

Looking for opportunities in the gap between subjective perception and objective reality is easier using the following seven key methods.

1. There is always a gap between subjective perception and objective reality. The question is not whether or not that gap exists. There is always a gap between the objective nature of reality and our human subjective ability to perceive it. The only question is whether or not we know how to leverage that gap to improve people's subjective impression of our position (1.2 Subobjective Positions)

2. We can change perceptions either through repackaging or reeducation. Repackaging simply puts known facts in a better context. Re-education is much more difficult since it means changing one set of perceptions into another.

3. Repackaging requires clarifying our position, its value, and how it has changed. This is done through the five techniques of getting agreement, pointing out trends, highlighting scarcity, authority approval, and asking for favors covered more extensively later in The Playbook (8.3.2 Distinctive Packaging).

4. Re-education requires communicating non-conforming facts that conflict with existing perceptions. Everyone thinks that their opinions are based upon facts, but perceptions usually come tfirst. After perceptions are formed, facts that don't conform to those perceptions are unconsciously filtered out. This is known scientifically as confirmation bias. It requires work to break down this bias (2.1.1 Information Limits).

5. We can only change opinions with facts not different opinions about facts. A non-conforming fact is not a different subjective interpretation of a fact. Nor can it be a piece of information that is questionable or debatable. It must be indisputably solid, but unnoticed. Pushing alternative opinions only creates reactance , people's desire to do the opposite of what they are pressured to do (2.3.1 Action and Reaction).

6. We must gather information to identify non-conforming facts that others do not see. We mistakenly think that others see the same fact that we do. Confirmation bias almost assures that others do not see what we see. Because of our different positions, we all have a different perspective. Our job is to identify what others are missing, which we do through the standard strategic technique for developing perspective (2.0 Developing Perspective).

7. We must present the non-confirming fact as surprising. If we do not draw attention to the fact as surprising, it will get filtered out through the normal process of confirmation bias. The fact may not seem surprising to us, but we must pretend that it is in order to communicate it. Surprise is always necessary when we want people to pay attention to what they would normally miss (2.1.4 Surprise).

Illustration:

As an illustration, let us examine the problem of getting someone to trust us. This is a common problem that comes up in a variety of both personal and professional issues of advancing a position.

1. There is always a gap between subjective perception and objective reality. People do not trust us because they know that they do not know us. We can never really know a person completely, but we can know them well enough to trust them.

2. We can change perceptions either through repackaging or reeducation. For our illustration, let us assume the problem is that we are known to be a little lazy. If its is true that we are a little lazy, we must repackage our laziness to its best advantage. If it is false, we must must work on reeducation.

3. Repackaging requires clarifying our position, its value, and how it has changed. The first step is clarifying the boundaries and benefits of our laziness. If we recognize that we are lazy in less important areas, we can claim to be prioritizing our efforts. We can also claim that one of the benefits is that our laziness has always spurred us to find more efficient and effective ways of working.

4. Re-education requires communicating non-conforming facts that conflict with existing perceptions. If we really are not lazy, the facts of our industriousness must exist.

5. We can only change opinions with facts not different opinions about facts. Here, we must make sure that we *are* really industrious and that we are not simply deluding ourselves.

6. We must gather information to identify non-conforming facts that others do not see. We must collect the date that proves how hard we work in measurable non-subjective terms: hours of work, number of tasks performed, etc.

7. We must present the non-confirming fact as surprising. If we just say, "You think I am lazy, but here are the facts," we will trigger reactance. However, if we start from a position of "Wow, I was surprised to find out that I did so much last month. I always thought I was pretty laid back about this stuff," we have a much better chance of being heard.

3.7.0 Redefining the Comparison

Description: Sun Tzu's eight key methods on redefining a competitive arena to create relative mismatches.

""You can divide the ground and still defend it."
Sun Tzu's The Art of War 6:3:15

"It was classic divide and conquer."
David Vise

General Principle: Competitors can be divided into different categories of comparison to uncover a hidden opening.

Situation:

Competition is based on making comparisons. The problem is that there are just some types of comparisons in which we are never going to look as good as we can. We get measured against the wrong competitors in the wrong ways. We can seem trapped by fate into comparison where we simply cannot stand out or rise up. In these situations, we cannot find openings. We are dominated by an environment in which we are a square peg in a world of round holes.

Opportunity:

Though opportunities are created by our environment, we can shape our environment by shaping how comparisons are made. How comparisons are made is based upon a subjective decision. This choice either divides one set of contestants or one set of judges from another. This choice defines the "battle ground". Sun Tzu described the battleground as infinite because it can be divided in an infinite number of ways. We can use division to reveal openings that don't exist from any standard perspective. When we cannot measure up on an existing yardstick, we may have the opportunity to invent new yardsticks for comparison. Yes, we must adapt to objective reality, conforming our strategy to real world conditions instead of trying to control them (3.2.1 Environmental Dominance). However, the subjective measures by which comparisons are made are infinitely variable.

Key Methods:

To redefine a competitive arena to produce more favorable comparisons, we must use the following key methods.

1. The way in which positions are compared is dynamic. People are always finding better ways to make comparisons. We can climb up the rungs of a ladder that already exists or we can reinvent the ladder. We make the choice based on how easily we can sell people on the idea of a new ladder where we already own a high rung. In the social sciences, framing describes the collection of concepts that people use to use understand and respond to events. We often have the ability to create new frames that divide that competitive space in innovative, new ways. We can then identify holes that are invisible from the ordinary ways in which those spaces are evaluated (1.1.1 Position Dynamics).

2. The opportunity for dividing the ground must exist in the environment. We cannot invent that ladder out of whole cloth. A new basis competition only works if others can easily see the value in a new framework for comparison. Those who judge must be rewarded in some way for using the new basis of comparison (3.1.2 Strategic Profitability),

3. We must understand the current basis for how our ground is currently divided. This means that we must have a broad perspective on our competitive arena. We must understand how the rankings within it are currently made and why (2.4.1 Ground Perspective).

4. List the characteristics that are currently used for comparison. What are the current methods of competitive comparison? This is, of course, different for every competitive arena. These are the common characteristics that bring a group of competitors, creating a specific competitive arena (1.3.1 Competitive Comparison).

5. List potential areas of comparison that are currently overlooked. There are four common ideas we can use for inspiration here: a) finer distinctions that create smaller groups, b) distinctions that make bigger groups, b) distinctions than emphasize change or rate of change rather than static conditions, and c) distinctions that are made in similar types of competitive arenas (2.6 Knowledge Leverage).

6. We identify overlooked characteristics that give us a clear advantage. We identify comparisons in which we can excel and in which others do well. These characteristics obviously emphasize our strengths. These depend upon our current position and our relative capabilities (3.5 Strength and Weakness).

7. There must be an advantage _for others_ in using our new yardstick. We want others to use this yardstick because it improves our position, but they will not use it unless it is in their best interests to do so. The new frame must help them understand the competitive arena better so that they can make better comparisons and choices. There are often empty niches for comparisons waiting to be filled. No one sees those niches because no one asks these questions. This potential for benefit in using a new yardstick has to exist in the situation, both for ourselves and for others. (1.6.1 Shared Mission).

8. *We must be able to promote the value of seeing the ground in this new way to others*. This goes back to the concept that we must make claims in order to get rewarded. A new yardstick does us no good unless we can get people to use it (8.2 Making Claims).

Illustration:

Let us illustrate these key methods by examining the positioning of a business in an existing marketplace.

1. *The way in which positions are compared is dynamic.* Since I personally prefer working in more dynamic competitive arenas, redefining ground is my preferred way of identifying openings and competing. Let us examine how I positioned my software company before I sold it.

2. *The opportunity for dividing the ground must exist in the environment.* We got into the software market because it was fast growing. Quickly growing competitive arenas create more opportunities for dividing the ground as more complexity emerges.

3. *We must understand the current basis for how our ground is currently divided.* Since we grew our company into our market niche for over a decade, we understood how the game was played.

4. *List the characteristics that are currently used for comparison.* In our area of software--order processing systems for large, multinational manufacturers, comparison was usually made on the basis of detailed feature sets. The purchasing decision was based on which software package had the best feature set.

5. *List potential areas of comparison that are currently overlooked.* We could have tried to go into more detailed descriptions of features, but the list was already beyond human comprehension. We could have looked at areas of computers, for example, Apple, and competed on the basis of a more exciting user interface.

6. We identify overlooked characteristics that give us a clear advantage. Our product was built to make it easy to tailor our product to meet specific needs. A concept that we called, modifiable-bydesign.

7. There must be an advantage <u>for others</u> in using our new yardstick. We changed the decision away from choosing software by comparing endless lists of competing features. Instead we asked if the potential customer wanted to a) adapt their business processes to fit the software and then freeze those processes or 2) adapt the software to fit their process and continue modifying the software as their business changed while retaining the ability to keep those modifications when they moved to a new version of the software.

8. We must be able to promote the value of seeing the ground in this new way to others. Needless to say, this was a fairly easy decision and we quickly became the number one accounting product on our platform, Unix servers. \

3.8.0t Strategic Matrix Analysis

Description: Sun Tzu's four key methods regarding two-dimensional representations of a strategic battleground.

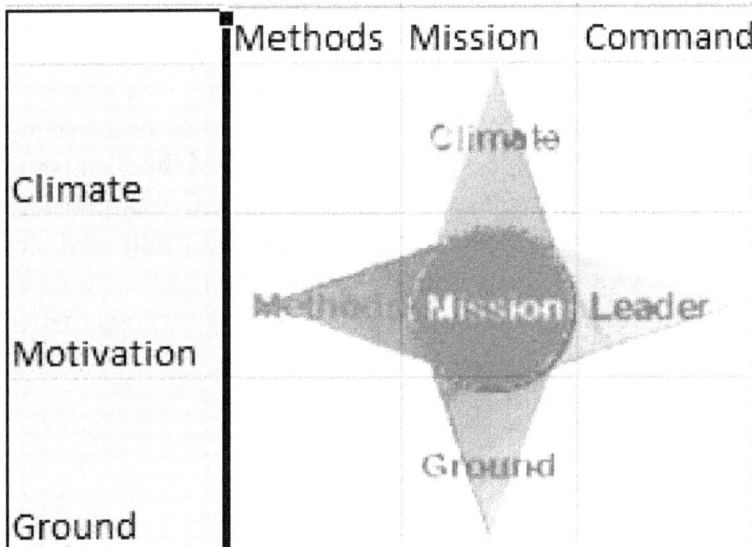

> *"You can recognize the opportunity for victory; you don't create it."*
>
> Sun Tzu's The Art of War 4:1:10

> *"There exist limitless opportunities in every industry. Where there is an open mind, there will always be a frontier."*
>
> Charles Kettering

General Principle: Mapping situations using the five elements in a matrix makes openings easier to see and predict.

Situation:

As we can see from this section of The Playbook, there are many types of openings and the concept of "openings" can get very conceptual. The problem is that, as humans, we are wired primarily for visual perception. When our methods are purely conceptual, we miss many of our potential opportunities because we cannot "see" the openings involved.

Opportunity:

One of the most sophisticated ways to discover openings is using Strategic Matrix Analysis. Strategic Matrix Analysis uses the Stratrix, a visual tool for helping people see the key relationships among a given set of competitors. The purpose of the Stratrix is to provide a two-dimensional representation of the five dimensions (mission/climate/ground/leader/methods) used in traditional strategic analysis. One of the primary ways we can use this tool is to map competitive arenas in order to identify the openings that create opportunities.

Key Methods:

There are many different uses of the Stratrix tool, but the purpose of this article is simply to introduce the tool and its use in discovering opportunities.

	Low Price	Quality	Custom
Novel			
Standard			
Mass			

1. The generic Stratrix is three-by-three, nine-celled matrix.
The three columns of the Stratrix represent the major components of an competitor: a) methods, b) specific mission, and c) command. The three rows of the stratrix represent the major components of the competitive environment: 1) climate, 2) general motivations, 3) ground. Following the normal compass map of the five key elements (1.3 Elemental Analysis).

2. The rows and columns are modified to reflect the unique *character of the competitive arena.* Since each of the five dimensions represented in the matrix has many different defining characteristics, a special Stratrix can be designed to compare only those characteristics seen as the most relevant in a given competitive situation. We usually use the matrix to organize the characteristics already used to divide groups of competitors in a given arena (3.7 Defining the Ground). In this version, we compare the positioning of various companies and products. The columns represent various types of sellers--a) low price, b) quality c) custom. The rows represent types of customer markets--1) the market for novelty, 3) the market for standards, 3) the mass market.

3. Relative competitive positions are mapped on the Stratrix.
The Matrix is used to map relative positions. Each relevant competitor will have both a location and take up a certain amount of "space" on the map. The space represents the mental space owned by the competitors. Using this tool, we can chart in two dimensions the positions that competitors occupy in five dimensions. This allows us to see their relative position to each other.

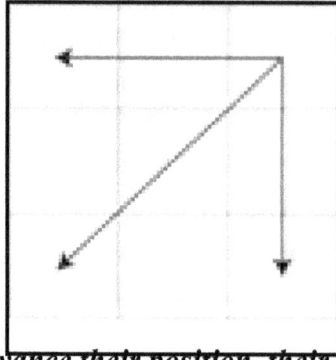

As competitors advance their position, their positions tend to move down and to the left. One important aspect of the Market Analysis Stratrix is that we can use it to predict the paths of competitors in a competitive arena. That path starts at the top, since new position are created by climate and moves down as they establish themselves on the ground. They also move from right to left, from command, making decision, to methods, as those methods become more established (1.1 Position Paths).

Illustration:

Let us say that there are three competitors in a market. Blue is a company like Apple sells cutting edge, high-quality products that have become standard in a few areas. Red appeals more to the standard and mass markets with combining quality and low price. Green focuses more on low price and standards.

	Low Price	Quality	Custom
Novel			
Standard			
Mass			

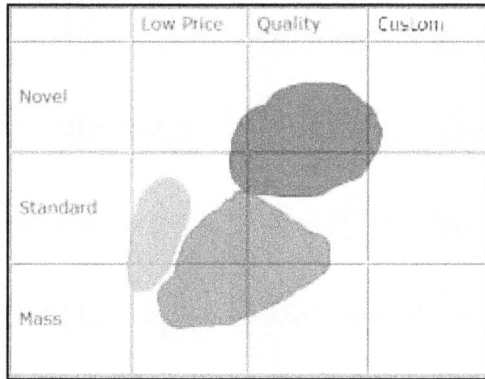

The question is, where is the potential opening? In real life, most people just look at the tiny openings between competitors: areas of quality that are missed by Blue and Red, the areas of standards missed by Red and Green. New competitors entering this market might even miss those tiny openings, instead going after areas already occupied by one of the major existing competitors. These "me-to" products would almost certainly fail because there is no opening and therefore, no opportunity.

The real potential openings in this market are the cells that are almost entirely empty for any type of more customized product or for a low-priced novel product. If a competitor can get to one of these positions, they know that they will not face competition in these areas. They cannot know the value of these positions before exploring them (3.1.5 Unpredictable Value), but they can know that this positions represent open ground.

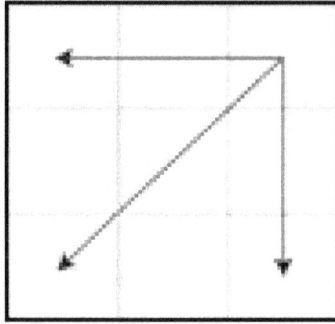

As these organizations develop and grow, they migrate from the upper right-hand corner down toward the lower left-hand cell. Blue sells very novel products today, but success makes it hard to maintain novelty. If successful, products that were once novel move into the mass market. Smart competitors enter markets in the upper right-hand box (very novel, custom products) taking the highground from existing products. Then, as they grow, their leading edge sucks the life of their competitions railing edge.

Glossary of Key Concepts from
Sun Tzu's *The Art of War*

This glossary is keyed to the most common English words used in the translation of *The Art of War*. Those terms only capture the strategic concepts generally. Though translated as English nouns, verbs, adverbs, or adjectives, the Chinese characters on which they are based are totally conceptual, not parts of speech. For example, the character for conflict is translated as the noun "conflict," as the verb "fight," and as the adjective "disputed." Ancient written Chinese was a conceptual language, not a spoken one. More like mathematical terms, these concepts are primarily defined by the strict structure of their relationships with other concepts. The Chinese names shown in parentheses with the characters are primarily based on Pinyin, but we occasionally use Cantonese terms to make each term unique.

Advance (*Jeun* 進): to move into new **ground**; to expand your **position**; to move forward in a campaign; the opposite of **flee**.

Advantage, *benefit* (*Li* 利): an opportunity arising from having a better **position** relative to an **enemy**; an opening left by an **enemy**; a **strength** that matches against an **enemy's weakness**; where fullness meets emptiness; a desirable characteristic of a strategic **position**.

Aim, *vision, foresee* (*Jian* 見): **focus** on a specific **advantage**, opening, or opportunity; predicting movements of an **enemy**; a skill of a **leader** in observing **climate**.

Analysis, *plan* (*Gai* 計): a comparison of relative **position**; the examination of the five factors that define a strategic **position**; a combination of **knowledge** and vision; the ability to see through **deception**.

Army: see **war.**

Attack, *invade* (*Gong* 攻): a movement to new **ground**; advancing a strategic **position**; action against an **enemy** in the sense of moving into his **ground**; opposite of **defend**; does not necessarily mean **conflict.**

Bad, *ruined* (*Pi* 圮): a condition of the **ground** that makes **advance** difficult; destroyed; terrain that is broken and difficult to traverse; one of the nine situations or types of terrain.

Barricaded: see **obstacles.**

Battle (*Zhan* 戰): to challenge; to engage an **enemy;** generically, to meet a challenge; to choose a confrontation with an **enemy** at a specific time and place; to focus all your resources on a task; to establish superiority in a **position**; to challenge an **enemy** to increase **chaos;** that which is **controlled** by **surprise;** one of the four forms of **attack;** the response to a **desperate situation;** character meaning was originally "big meeting," though later took on the meaning "big weapon"; not necessarily conflict.

Bravery, *courage* (*Yong* 勇): the ability to face difficult choices; the character quality that deals with the changes of **CLIMATE;** courage of conviction; willingness to act on vision; one of the six characteristics of a leader.

Break, *broken, divided* (*Po* 破): to **divide** what is **complete**; the absence of a **uniting philosophy**; the opposite of <u>unity</u>.

Calculate, *count* (*Shu* 数): mathematical comparison of quantities and qualities; a measurement of **distance** or troop size.

Change, *transform* (*Bian* 變): transition from one **condition** to another; the ability to adapt to different situations; a natural characteristic of **climate**.

Chaos, *disorder* (*Juan* 亂): **conditions** that cannot be **foreseen**; the natural state of confusion arising from **battle**; one of six weaknesses of an organization; the opposite of **control**.

Claim, *position, form* (*Xing* 形): to use the **ground**; a shape or specific condition of **ground**; the **ground** that you **control**; to use the benefits of the **ground**; the formations of troops; one of the four key skills in making progress.

Climate, *heaven* (*Tian* 天): the passage of time; the realm of uncontrollable **change**; divine providence; the weather; trends that **change** over time; generally, the future; what one must **aim** at in the future; one of five key factors in **analysis;** the opposite of **ground**.

Command (*Ling* 令): to order or the act of ordering subordinates; the decisions of a **leader**; the creation of **methods**.

Competition: see <u>war.</u>

Complete: see <u>unity.</u>

Condition: see **ground.**

Confined, *surround* (*Wei* 圍): to encircle; a **situation** or **stage** in which your options are limited; the proper tactic for dealing with an **enemy** that is ten times smaller; to seal off a smaller **enemy**; the characteristic of a **stage** in which a larger **force** can be attacked by a smaller one; one of nine **situations** or **stages**.

Conflict, *fight* (*Zheng* 爭): to contend; to dispute; direct confrontation of arms with an **enemy**; highly desirable **ground** that creates disputes; one of nine types of **ground,** terrain, or stages.

Constricted, *narrow* (*Ai* 狹): a confined space or niche; one of six field positions; the limited extreme of the dimension distance; the opposite of **spread-out**.

Control, *govern* (*Chi* 治): to manage situations; to overcome disorder; the opposite of **chaos**.

Dangerous: see **serious.**

Dangers, *adverse* (Ak 阨): a condition that makes it difficult to **advance**; one of three dimensions used to evaluate advantages; the dimension with the extreme field **positions** of **entangling** and **supporting**.

Death, *desperate* (Si 死): to end or the end of life or efforts; an extreme situation in which the only option is **battle**; one of nine **stages** or types of **terrain**; one of five types of **spies**; opposite of **survive**.

Deception, *bluffing, illusion* (Gui 詭): to control perceptions; to control information; to mislead an **enemy**; an attack on an opponent's **aim**; the characteristic of war that confuses perceptions.

Defend (Shou 守): to guard or to hold a **ground**; to remain in a **position**; the opposite of **attack**.

Detour (Yu 迂): the indirect or unsuspected path to a **position**; the more difficult path to **advantage**; the route that is not **direct**.

Direct, *straight* (Jik 直): a straight or obvious path to a goal; opposite of **detour**.

Distance, *distant* (Yuan 遠): the space separating **ground**; to be remote from the current location; to occupy **positions** that are not close to one another; one of six field positions; one of the three dimensions for evaluating opportunities; the emptiness of space.

Divide, *separate* (Fen 分): to break apart a larger force; to separate from a larger group; the opposite of **join** and **focus**.

Double agent, *reverse* (Fan 反): to turn around in direction; to change a situation; to switch a person's allegiance; one of five types of spies.

Easy, *light* (Qing 輕): to require little effort; a **situation** that requires little effort; one of nine **stages** or types of terrain; opposite of **serious**.

Emotion, *feeling* (Xin 心): an unthinking reaction to **aim**, a necessary element to inspire **moves**; a component of esprit de corps; never a sufficient cause for **attack**.

Enemy, *competitor* (Dik 敵): one who makes the same **claim**; one with a similar **goal**; one with whom comparisons of capabilities are made.

Entangling, *hanging* (Gua 懸): a **position** that cannot be returned to; any **condition** that leaves no easy place to go; one of six field positions.

Evade, *avoid* (Bi 避): the tactic used by small competitors when facing large opponents.

Fall apart, *collapse* (Beng 崩): to fail to execute good decisions; to fail to use a **constricted position**; one of six weaknesses of an organization.

Fall down, *sink* (Haam 陷): to fail to make good decisions; to **move** from a **supporting position**; one of six weaknesses of organizations.

Feelings, *affection, love* (_Ching_ 情): the bonds of relationship; the result of a shared **philosophy**; requires management.

Fight, *struggle* (Dou 鬥): to engage in **conflict**; to face difficulties.

Fire (_Huo_ 火): an environmental weapon; a universal analogy for all weapons.

Flee, *retreat, northward* (_Bei_ 北): to abandon a **position**; to surrender **ground**; one of six weaknesses of an **army**; opposite of **advance**.

Focus, *concentrate* (_Zhuan_ 專): to bring resources together at a given time; to **unite** forces for a purpose; an attribute of having a shared **philosophy**; the opposite of *divide*.

Force (_Lei_ 力): power in the simplest sense; a **group** of people bound by **unity** and **focus**; the relative balance of **strength** in opposition to **weakness**.

Foresee: see **aim**.

Fullness: see **strength**.

General: see **leader**.

Goal: see **philosophy**.

Ground, *situation, stage* (_Di_ 地): the earth; a specific place; a specific condition; the place one competes; the prize of competition; one of five key factors in competitive analysis; the opposite of **climate**.

Groups, *troops* (_Dui_ 隊): a number of people united under a shared **philosophy**; human resources of an organization; one of the five targets of fire attacks.

Inside, *internal* (_Nei_ 內): within a **territory** or organization; an insider; one of five types of spies; opposite of _Wai_, outside.

Intersecting, *highway* (_Qu_ 衢): a **situation** or **ground** that allows you to **join**; one of nine types of terrain.

Join (_Hap_ 合): to unite; to make allies; to create a larger **force**; opposite of **divide**.

Knowledge, *listening* (_Zhi_: 知): to have information; the result of listening; the first step in advancing a **position**; the basis of strategy.

Lax, *loosen* (_Shii_ 弛): too easygoing; lacking discipline; one of six weaknesses of an army.

Leader, *general, commander* (_Jiang_ 將): the decision-maker in a competitive unit; one who **listens** and **aims**; one who manages **troops**; superior of officers and men; one of the five key factors in analysis; the conceptual opposite of _fa_, the established methods, which do not require decisions.

Learn, *compare* (_Xiao_ 效): to evaluate the relative qualities of **enemies**.

Listen, *obey* (_Ting_ 聽): to gather **knowledge**; part of **analysis**.

Listening: see **knowledge**.

Local, *countryside* (*Xiang* 鄉): the nearby **ground**; to have **knowledge** of a specific **ground**; one of five types of **spies**.

Marsh (*Ze* 澤): **ground** where footing is unstable; one of the four types of **ground**; analogy for uncertain situations.

Method: see **system**.

Mission: see **philosophy**.

Momentum, *influence* (*Shi* 勢): the **force** created by **surprise** set up by **standards**; used with **timing**.

Mountains, *hill, peak* (*Shan* 山): uneven **ground**; one of four types of **ground**; an analogy for all unequal **situations**.

Move, *march, act* (*Hang* 行): action toward a position or goal; used as a near synonym for *dong*, act.

Nation (*Guo* 國): the state; the productive part of an organization; the seat of political power; the entity that controls an **army** or competitive part of the organization.

Obstacles, *barricaded* (*Xian* 險): to have barriers; one of the three characteristics of the **ground**; one of six field positions; as a field position, opposite of **unobstructed**.

Open, *meeting, crossing* (*Jiao* 來): to share the same **ground** without conflict; to come together; a **situation** that encourages a race; one of nine **terrains** or **stages**.

Opportunity: see *advantage.*

Outmaneuver (*Sou* 走): to go astray; to be **forced** into a **weak position**; one of six weaknesses of an army.

Outside, *external* (*Wai* 外): not within a **territory** or **army**; one who has a different perspective; one who offers an objective view; opposite of **internal**.

Philosophy, *mission, goals* (*Tao* 道): the shared **goals** that **unite** an **army**; a system of thought; a shared viewpoint; literally "the way"; a way to work together; one of the five key factors in **analysis**.

Plateau (*Liu* 陸): a type of **ground** without defects; an analogy for any equal, solid, and certain **situation**; the best place for competition; one of the four types of **ground**.

Resources, *provisions* (*Liang* 糧): necessary supplies, most commonly food; one of the five targets of fire attacks.

Restraint: see **timing.**

Reward, *treasure, money* (_Bao_ 賞): profit; wealth; the necessary compensation for competition; a necessary ingredient for **victory**; **victory** must pay.

Scatter, *dissipating* (_San_ 散): to disperse; to lose **unity**; the pursuit of separate **goals** as opposed to a central **mission**; a situation that causes a **force** to scatter; one of nine conditions or types of terrain.

Serious, *heavy* (_Chong_ 重): any task requiring effort and skill; a **situation** where resources are running low when you are deeply committed to a campaign or heavily invested in a project; a situation where opposition within an organization mounts; one of nine **stages** or types of **terrain**.

Siege (_Gong Cheng_ 攻城): to move against entrenched positions; any movement against an **enemy's strength**; literally "strike city"; one of the four forms of attack; the least desirable form of attack.

Situation: see **ground.**

Speed, *hurry* (Sai 馳): to **move** over **ground** quickly; the ability to **advance positions** in a minimum of time; needed to take advantage of a window of opportunity.

Spread-out, *wide* (_Guang_ 廣): a surplus of **distance**; one of the six **ground positions**; opposite of **constricted.**

Spy, *conduit, go-between* (_Gaan_ 間): a source of information; a channel of communication; literally, an "opening between."

Stage: see **ground.**

Standard, *proper, correct* (_Jang_ 正): the expected behavior; the standard approach; proven methods; the opposite of surprise; together with **surprise** creates **momentum.**

Storehouse, *house* (_Ku_ 庫): a place where resources are stockpiled; one of the five targets for fire attacks.

Stores, *accumulate, savings* (_Ji_ 糧):resources that have been stored; any type of inventory; one of the five targets of fire attacks.

Strength,*fullness, satisfaction* (_Sat_ 壹): wealth or abundance or resources; the state of being crowded; the opposite of Xu, empty.

Supply wagons, *transport* (_Zi_ 輜): the movement of **resources** through **distance**; one of the five targets of fire attacks.

Support, *supporting* (_Zhii_ 支): to prop up; to enhance; a **ground position** that you cannot leave without losing **strength**; one of six field positions; the opposite extreme of gua, entangling.

Surprise, *unusual, strange* (*Qi* 奇) : the unexpected; the innovative; the opposite of **standard**; together with **standards** creates **momentum**.

Surround: see **confined**.

Survive, *live, birth* (*Shaang* 生): the state of being created, started, or beginning; the state of living or surviving; a temporary condition of fullness; one of five types of spies; the opposite of **death**.

System, *method* (*Fa* 法): a set of procedures; a group of techniques; steps to accomplish a **goal**; one of the five key factors in analysis; the realm of groups who must follow procedures; the opposite of the **leader**.

Territory, *terrain*: see **ground**.

Timing, *restraint* (*Jie* 節): to withhold action until the proper time; to release tension; a companion concept to **momentum**.

Troops: see **group**.

Unity, *whole, oneness* (*Yi* 一): the characteristic of a **group** that shares a **philosophy**; the lowest number; a **group** that acts as a unit; the opposite of **divided**.

Unobstructed, *expert* (*Tong* 通): without obstacles or barriers; **ground** that allows easy movement; open to new ideas; one of six field positions; opposite of **obstructed**.

Victory, *win, winning* (*Sing* 勝): success in an endeavor; getting a reward; serving your mission; an event that produces more than it consumes; to make a profit.

War, *competition, army* (Bing 兵): a dynamic situation in which **positions** can be won or lost; a contest in which a **reward** can be won; the conditions under which the principles of strategy work.

Water, *river* (*Shui* 水): a fast-changing **ground**; fluid **conditions**; one of four types of **ground**; an analogy for change.

Weakness, *emptiness, need* (*Xu* 虛): the absence of people or resources; devoid of **force**; the point of **attack** for an **advantage;** a characteristic of **ground** that enables **speed**; poor; the opposite of strength.

Win, *winning*: see **victory**.

Wind, *fashion, custom* (*Feng* 風): the pressure of environmental forces.

The *Art of War Playbook* Series

There are over two-hundred and thirty articles on Sun Tzu's competitive principles in the nine volumes of the *Art of War Playbook*. Each volume covers a specific area of Sun Tzu strategy.

About the Translator and Author

Gary Gagliardi is recognized as America's leading expert on Sun Tzu's *The Art of War*. An award-winning author and business strategist, his many books on Sun Tzu's strategy have been translated around the world. He has appeared on hundreds of talk shows nationwide, providing strategic insight on the breaking news. He has trained decision makers from some of the world's most successful organizations in competitive thinking. His workshops convert Sun Tzu's many principles into a series of practical tools for handling common competitive challenges.

Gary began using Sun Tzu's competitive principles in a successful corporate career and when he started his own software company. In 1990, he wrote his first *Art of War* adaptation for his company's salespeople. By 1992, his company was on *Inc. Magazine's* list of the 500 fastest-growing privately held companies in America. He personally won the U.S. Chamber of Commerce Blue Chip Quality Award and was an Ernst and Young Entrepreneur of the Year finalist. His customers—AT&T, GE, and Motorola, among others—began inviting him to speak at their conferences. After becoming a multimillionaire when he sold his software company in 1997, he continued teaching *The Art of War* around the world.

Gary has authored several breakthrough works on *The Art of War*. Ten of his books on strategy have won book award recognition in nine different non-fiction categories.

Other *Art of War* Books
by Gary Gagliardi

9 FORMULAS FOR BUSINESS SUCCESS:
THE SCIENCE OF STRATEGY

THE GOLDEN KEY TO STRATEGY:
EVERYDAY STRATEGY FOR EVERYONE

SUN TZU'S THE ART OF WAR PLUS THE ART OF SALES:
THE ART OF WAR FOR THE SALES WARRIOR

SUN TZU'S THE ART OF WAR PLUS THE ART OF SALES:
THE ART OF WAR FOR THE SALES WARRIOR

THE ART OF WAR PLUS THE CHINESE REVEALED

THE ART OF WAR PLUS THE ART OF MANAGEMENT:
THE ART OF WAR FOR MANAGEMENT WARRIORS

THE ART OF WAR PLUS THE ART OF MANAGEMENT:
THE ART OF WAR FOR MANAGEMENT WARRIORS

MAKING MONEY BY SPEAKING:
THE SPOKESPERSON STRATEGY

THE WARRIOR CLASS:
306 LESSONS IN STRATEGY

THE ART OF WAR FOR THE BUSINESS WARRIOR:
STRATEGY FOR ENTREPRENEURS

THE ART OF WAR PLUS THE WARRIOR'S APPRENTICE

THE ART OF WAR PLUS STRATEGY FOR SALES MANAGERS

ART OF WAR FOR WARRIOR MARKETING:
STRATEGY FOR CONQUERING MARKETS

THE ANCIENT BING-FA:
MARTIAL ARTS STRATEGY

STRATEGY AGAINST TERROR:
ANCIENT WISDOM FOR TODAY'S WAR

THE ART OF WAR PLUS THE ART OF CAREER BUILDING

THE ART OF PARENTING:
SUN TZU'S ART OF WAR FOR PARENTING TEENS

Gary Gagliardi's Books are Available at:

SunTzus.com
Amazon.com
BarnesAndNoble.com
Itunes.apple.com

www.ingramcontent.com/pod-product-compliance
Lightning Source LLC
Chambersburg PA
CBHW071845200326
41519CB00016B/4238